Expected End

What Culture Is, Why It Matters
and How to Improve it

Mike Friesen

FIRST EDITION

The stories in this book are true but the names and call signs
are changed to protect the privacy of those involved.

ISBN 978-0-6152-1563-1

Acknowledgements

To my beautiful wife who patiently listened to many hours of monologue knowing just when to insert her natural frankness and ask insightful questions. She also read and edited countless draft letters, papers, articles, and finally this book.

Thank you to my sons who helped shape this book. Piercingly honest conversations with the boys created the sections on counsel and encouragement and caused new learning in me. Other refinements came through fun brainstorming and their willingness to pull their weight as part of our family team.

Thank you to Lee Hawkins who persistently coached me through many paradigm shifts to really see what is possible and helped me develop a wide range of process tools. I often think of his question at critical decision making points: "What does your heart say?"

I greatly appreciate Dr. Bob Finkelmeier's help in reviewing and editing this book. I first met Dr. Bob while enrolled in the Western Governors University M.B.A. program and quickly came to value his thoroughly wise approach to teaching.

Contents

Introduction

"Mike, would you present the vision, mission, and values statement of your finance department at our semi-annual conference later this month?"

"Will do, sir," I replied.

The good Colonel hung up and I swallowed hard because my co-workers and I had not so much as touched the subject of a mission statement. Although the words were familiar, I was clueless on the concepts. My mind raced as I pondered how to tackle this assignment. What was the difference between a vision and a mission? How would I pick the most important values and would they represent the office staff ideals? How much should I involve the staff with the short deadline?

Ironically, as a new Chief Financial Officer, I had this gnawing sensation of needing to lead the office team somewhere and indirectly influence the organization as a whole. (So I have keen sense for the obvious.) We were struggling with travel expense reimbursement turnaround time, our payroll results were somewhat spotty and the accounting systems were overly difficult. The good news was we had highly experienced and dedicated individuals in the office who wanted to make a difference.

As a long-time military member and fighter pilot, I was accustomed to the idea of mission in the sense of protecting a ground or airborne asset or denying the enemy access to flight lanes, etc. The presentation agreement with the Colonel was different. What was our bottom line mission as a finance department? Where should we be going? Was our mission to simply follow orders and pay the bills? What about all the areas I was realizing needed improvement?

I made a phone call to our Director of Quality and we began what would be a series of long conversations over the next few years. First, he helped me craft a response to the immediate assignment from the Colonel. Second, and more importantly, the director was much more interested in exploring the process to help me understand the concepts behind the words. The more I studied these and other ideas, the more I recognized a severe lack of personal knowledge and experience in the matter of leadership thought and cultural change.

Prior to this time, my definition of leadership was "taking initiative" and culture was a societal thing like a country or something you found in a lab. This was plain, simple and shallow. The only other thought was how the word leadership had a nice ring to it and seemed to give honor by its very usage. For instance, senior members of our organization were described as "senior leaders." High ranking political officials were always known as world leaders (not supervisors, bosses or managers). In other words, the concept of leadership was a superficial idea in my mind.

So began a journey that would make many twists and turns and is still progressing to this day. I am so grateful to the military for sending me through several professional development classes which greatly helped my understanding. Through a variety of lengthy discussions with coaches and mentors, classes, books, seminars, live experience and hard knocks, leadership theory and change began to take on a life all its own. A new world was (and still is) opening up and it was all taking on a context as culture.

Light Bulb Moments

There are many memorable moments including the time I phoned my leadership coach shortly after an extended discussion. One of his strengths was asking great questions and today had been no exception. We often started our discussions in a safe and predictable place only to wander far afield in search of new paradigms and conceptual muscle-flexing. My conventional pattern is to chew on a topic long after the actual conversation stops. This day was no different.

As I pulled into the parking lot of a local restaurant, a light bulb snapped on in my head. I quickly dialed the coach's number.

"Are you saying disagreement and disrespect are two separate things," I asked?

"Yes, you got it," was his reply. "Now, write an article on what you have learned."

I presented the article a few days later and this process and follow-on discussion reinforced the important points. How could such a basic point have eluded me all the preceding years? I may never know the answer to that question but the point was to move forward and build on this learning. I slowly began to realize leadership growth was a competition with self to be a life-long student and learner.

Organizational Diagnosis

Another significant point in my leadership journey occurred while spending a week with several senior members of a military organization. A highly skilled consultant led us through a model of organizational diagnosis and design that generated many questions and new insights. There was much honest debate and a newfound recognition of current reality in our organization. The conclusions resonated and we knew they were at least 80% solutions.

This business of examining an enterprise, much like a doctor reading x-rays of a broken bone, was absolutely fascinating. As we rolled through the week, I expected my military unit to embrace the obvious recommendations and move forward with creativity and innovation. The excitement among some of us who were more junior and naïve was obvious. I volunteered for a follow-on committee assignment and enthusiastically jumped into the process with both feet.

Our group met a few times but fell into a predictable pattern of trying to please the bosses followed by apathetic resignation. Within a few weeks, it was apparent no real improvement would surface and this was very disappointing. I stopped attending the group meetings shortly thereafter. I was puzzled as to how to make a difference as there had been much talk with precious little change. I continued to refine my own point of view on leadership by attempting various initiatives within the finance directorate where I was in charge. Honestly, there were mixed results in the early stages but I had no regrets at blundering in with this new-found knowledge.

People Are People

Since then, I have experienced other organizational cultures and arrived at the profound thought, "people are people" regardless of the organization. Each environment has its own unique characteristics and quirks and yet human needs, desires and behaviors are relatively constant.

In the military, a common response to cultural change attempts was "You can't do that here; this is the military." Sounded plausible the first time I heard it but the sentiment quickly turned hollow. This reaction was actually a thinly disguised way to justify status quo methods and avoid the hard mental work of change.

Since then I have heard virtually the same words in other non-profit and for-profit settings. Every enterprise is beset by one form or another of cumbersome laws, rules and informal methods that make change difficult. As a result, it is natural to be intimidated by the obstacles to achieving a healthier culture. In an organizational sense, people behave very consistently regardless of business or agency type.

Perhaps you have heard something similar? "You can't do that here; that stuff is for _____ (fill in the blank with someone else's name, company or industry). As the old saying goes, when we designate a vague someone to do something, nobody usually winds up doing it.

The aim of this book is to relay common sense ideas in the pursuit of healthier cultures. There is no magic cure for what ails a company but there are concrete ways in which to move in a positive direction. While many of the ideas in this book use business and aviation illustrations, the concepts are just as applicable to other cultures as well such as a couple, a family, a volunteer team or business. It goes along with another comment I heard recently: "I just want to work at a happy place."

> **In an organizational sense, people behave very consistently regardless of business or agency type.**

Well said. There are countless employees, entrepreneurs, family members, volunteers and the like who long for a happier place to give their efforts. They are working their hearts out but are enduring dysfunctional cultures of assorted dimensions. There are many well-intentioned bosses who want to make things better but are unsure of where to start.

Culture and Results

Along the culture journey, I had the chance to work with a mentor on process improvement in a sister division. The discussions were filled with energy as the members were very motivated to contribute. This mentor had built a high-trust setting where it was acceptable to give honest input. The conversations were amazing and enlightening.

We had some wonderful participants in the dialogue who were especially good at questioning assumptions. We carefully diagnosed and then moved to prescription with a constant eye to vision, mission and principled values. The section eventually realized a significant improvement in financial service by greatly reducing turnaround time on travel reimbursement. This was no small thing given the unwieldy government systems in use.

Results matter but culture matters more. Yes, the company must produce to remain in business. Yes, the non-profit needs to continue giving service to stay viable. The question is not whether we should have products that will sell *or* company culture that inspires but we should achieve both because there is no escaping the fact that culture drives the output.

Several years ago, as a member of a small, geographically separated military unit of two dozen or so, I saw the amazing results from great culture and outstanding service. Our responsibility was to keep two F-15s on alert duty as part of the national defense network. Aircraft in this status are ready to launch at a moment's notice in response to direct threats to the continental United States.

One of the hallmarks of this unit culture was a willingness by all members to do any task required to meet the mission without regard to job descriptions. There was plenty of humor combined with a steady commitment to around-the-clock readiness. I marveled time after time at the disciplined yet enjoyable activity that permitted alert pilots to routinely fly training missions while posted to 48-hour alert shifts and remain ready for an alert call.

When the inevitable mechanical breakdown would occur, the unit members would respond as one. Sometimes, we needed extra creativity and commitment to procure replacement parts. At other times, we needed unconventional thought in dealing with higher headquarter demands while repairing a sick bird and maintaining our status. In all, we produced great service based on an excellent work culture.

There were significant elements that made it possible to have an above average culture at this unit.

- A positional leader (Commander) who cultivated an environment where we were expected to speak our minds
- Team members who would have given their thoughts whether the Commander wanted it or not
- Concern among and for each of the members beyond the traditional work environment
- A willingness to go against tradition for tradition sake in order to meet mission requirements; some delighted in questioning paradigms
- Professional relations with external agencies

It is important for any student of organizational climate to understand genuine attempts at cultural change count even when the near-term health may not be perfect. People recognize intent and will be more forgiving if they see good initiatives in progress.

The Future

Both results and culture are always interconnected and influence each other constantly. One will never be present without the other but culture ultimately determines the output. The person who looks only at results with little or no concern for culture is falling very short of the results that are otherwise possible. *Expected End* looks at the interplay of cultural elements and business output and how to improve culture and consequently improve results. The model also seeks to represent the relationship between all the elements of the cultural surroundings and how we must honor the process in order to have a product of which we can be proud.

A poor or mediocre company can produce results for a time but in our era of increasing competition, average will not go the distance. The global pressures are too great for any other outcome. For the organization seeking great results, culture based on principles will make the difference between long-term profitability or failure. Said another way, if you desire outstanding, long-term results, focus on all aspects of culture first and the results will happen naturally. This is all part of natural consequences to timeless principles.

Full Disclosure

This book is the product of a personal leadership adventure spanning nearly ten years that included countless resources like books, magazines, workshops, seminars, lectures, multi-media, mentor discussions, journal entries, book reports and first-hand experiences. The stories come from many more years in work, social and volunteer environments. I have been more fortunate than I could have expected and am grateful for the variety of experiences and stops along the way. Some of the learning came easier by observing great minds and hearts at work. Other lessons occurred despite fighting the inevitable hard knocks. The model on which this book rests is my subjective idea based on the many personal data points. My hope is this book proves helpful in the many environments where people are longing to better understand and improve corporate culture or desire to create outstanding cultures from scratch.

Chapter 1

Overview

Developing a highly effective culture requires the teamwork of several factors. Some elements are critical and others are less so. Leadership thinking is an important part as well. So often, we perceive leadership as a position but please be clear about the definition of leadership in this book (except where otherwise noted). Leadership is a way of thinking, a principled approach to life with a healthy respect for the long-term and a rabid focus on building trust. Leadership is about what goes on in the heart, the head, and the overall system and not just about a nameplate on the door. Leadership is much, much more than a position and we do the concept injustice by limiting it to those who occupy corner offices.

Why Culture Matters

Culture matters because it is present in all organizations. This fact is true regardless of size or type of family, group, organization or country. Not only is culture always present, it determines output. The output may be a product or a service or some combination thereof. The results may be as tangible as producing a measurable number of widgets or as intangible as improving someone's spiritual life. All along the spectrum, culture matters.

Further, culture determines the intrinsic value of the daily lives of people. Intrinsic things can be harder to measure and therefore tempting to dismiss as less useful. And yet, think about someone in your life you highly respect and name the top three reasons why. In most cases, the reasons will revolve around relational intrinsic perceptions such as these examples.

> **Leadership is a way of thinking, a principled approach to life with a healthy respect for the long-term and a rabid focus on building trust.**

"I always knew where he stood."

"She always valued my opinion."

"He believed in me."

Respect, team spirit, inspiration, motivation and other traits are not easily measured in a spreadsheet but are very powerful just the same.

Now applying this to an organization, cultures with higher intrinsic value are naturally more motivating to those involved. If your culture adds values to your employees and customers intrinsically, you can bet your bottom line they will add significant value to your business or non-profit agency results as well. This in turn contributes to your quality and longevity as an organization.

What Culture Creates

Culture creates a natural outcome, an expected end. Every culture does this and there are predictable, long-term results. Do not be fooled by short-term results when assessing culture as the true consequences often take more time to develop. A new but dysfunctional model may be bragged upon as the new and improved way to do business. An old but tired model may be enshrined while results have all but disappeared. Either way, there is a predictable outcome and the predictability comes by measuring against timeless principles (covered in more depth later). These natural and external laws impact all human relationships and are true from generation to generation. As sophisticated as we may become or as technologically savvy as we think we may be, we never get beyond the reach of timeless principles and their predictable consequences.

How to Improve Culture

One natural human tendency is to search for areas of comfort at least in relationships. How else could we explain why most people have friends of one sort or another? Whether introverted or extroverted, we all want relationships. There are areas of common interests that draw people together and, at times, push them apart. Because of this momentum toward comfortable relationships, culture is greatly impacted. The comfort level in many organizations is to find a "normal" way to do business and then stick with it. The old saying of, "If it isn't broken, don't fix it" paints the picture well. The problem is that technique and method effectiveness are short-lived. To improve a culture means to first cultivate an environment that values the overarching reasons of its very existence. This is not just what we produce or serve but is the long-term purpose. Looking at culture forces us to consider why we exist and then look for ways to continue meeting needs around this purpose by responding to our internal and external customers and the marketplace at large.

A leadership student's focus is on culture at all levels and the path to a premium environment requires five elements that make up the core of this book presented as a simple model below. The entry point is always at "Mindsets."

1. Discover, examine and modify **mindsets**. This opens a new way to *see*.

2. Develop **theories** to respond to these new and improved paradigms. This creates a new way to *think*.

3. Employ **application** of the theory in the real world to test and refine the assumptions. Application should be incremental as appropriate for the situation and include disciplined conflict. This produces a new way to *act*.

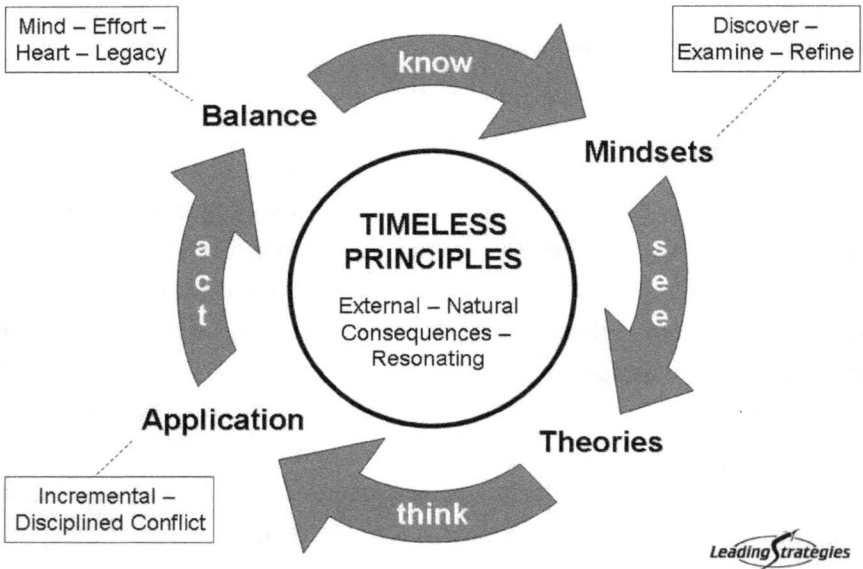

4. Strive for **balance** across life, family, team and organization by including the four elements of balance: mind, effort, heart and legacy. This results in an improved way to *know*.

5. Build and maintain a strong sense of **timeless principles** and make these the basis for all decision making. This is the permanent and predictable foundation.

The process as shown in the picture above of moving around the circle from see to think to act to know is a simple yet powerful roadmap for any leadership thinker to use in influencing culture. Each step builds upon the previous stage and sustained cultural improvement will not happen if any piece is skipped or neglected. Leave out seeing and the thinking will be small-minded. Ignore the thinking and the application will be haphazard. Disregard balance and the enterprise will struggle over the long-term to sustain results.

Stage 1 – Mindsets

Mindsets are always the entry point for growth in the *Expected End* model. Yes, always. If we do not consider mindsets, everything else is short-term behavior modification at best and pointless academics at the worst. Without a paradigm discussion, real growth, improvement and change are wishful thinking and the list of frustrating workplace problems will remain mostly unchanged. Without openness to mindset possibilities, creative ideas never see the light of day, application is rote and balance is impossible.

We look to our environments through mindsets, never around, under or over them. Ironically, the most comfortable mindsets are invisible so this calls for more work to uncover the hidden treasure maps. Exercising openness to the environment is an essential way to learn and grow. In short, it is critical to *see* first in order to *think*.

Stage 2 – Theories

Upon developing improved mindsets, the second step in the *Expected End* model is to move on to theories. Based on what you see so far, what do you think will happen? What are the nuts-and-bolts required to advance your supposition? How do you anticipate making the premise work? How will you evaluate the success or failure of your theory? These and many other questions are all part of fleshing out an adequate theory that moves us to the next step of application. Put another way, this is the planning stage.

As student pilots, instructors sometimes told us, "this is technique only" meaning there is more than one way to accomplish a task. Take the example of landing an airplane.

There are any number of ways to complete this assignment and different pilots define the outcome differently. However, there are also basics that apply to each landing such as not damaging the aircraft or yourself. On the method side, just ask a Navy pilot about an ideal carrier landing and then compare to an airline pilot's ideal arrival. One slams down and one kisses the ground. Neither is better than the other but serves a particular set of needs.

In the context of the *Expected End* model, a pilot needs to *see* the landing environment to *think* about what the essentials are and how to accomplish them. In order to *act* in a more generic sense, we must first *see* and then *think*. It is common sense to consider but more demanding to execute.

Stage 3 – Application

Regardless of what we think, the real world has a way of cutting through the clutter. The third step in *Expected End* is application. Most of us have had the disappointing experience of an idea proving less than workable in function despite how well it sounded in concept. Getting real through application is an important step in the path of building notable cultures as this step is the true refiner of great ideas. Reality is one of the allies in building outstanding climates within organizations.

We have probably all noticed how someone who is very good at something usually makes it look easy. There is nothing quite like experience with its dynamics and pratfalls. It was one thing to see and think about how to ride a bike and another to do it. On one of my first solo bike rides as a child, I forgot how to stop and chose to run into the side of a concrete building rather than coast out into a busy street. While this incident is laughable now, it is also typical of growing and learning. Mistakes are inevitable. Application shines a bright light on the mindsets and theories to aid in evaluation and improvement.

Stage 4 – Balance

In the zeal of thinking and doing, do not neglect balance, the fourth part of the model. Life is too short to waste in a productive yet unbalanced approach. And really, how productive is out-of-balance? I have attended a number of military retirement ceremonies. Invariably, there is mention of the standout achievements by the retiree and these are often significant. However, the highest impact moments in the ceremony happen when the words and thoughts turn toward relationships. The stories between and about people have much greater impact than the narratives about things.

Make a difference, leave a profound legacy and be sure someone has something honestly nice to say at your funeral. Balance: this makes or breaks the quality of life and will determine how robust the application is over the long-term.

At the Core – Timeless Principles

Timeless principles play a pivotal role in developing an undeniable level of effectiveness and form the core of the *Expected End* model. Without this core, the theory of this book collapses. We need some sort of standard on which to base decisions and there are a dizzying number from which to choose. For our purposes, this book will use timeless principles accepted by most healthy societies worldwide.

Timeless principles are outside our control and examples include excellence, respect, integrity, kindness, loyalty, commitment, honesty, service, humor, and forgiveness. Living by these and other related principles yield predictable, positive consequences. Neglecting these principles will also give predictable but negative results. These timeless rules are external to each of us and not subject to our tinkering.

Our mindsets, theories, actions and results will all be directly influenced by our foundation. The most interesting point is whether we choose to align with principles or not, the long-term outcomes are predictable every time. A key point is that the cultural model at the center of this book only stands strong through the use of timeless principles. Without principles, the model reverts to just another technique that will work once in a while. Please be clear about this: successful progression through the cultural model of *Expected End* requires alignment with the maximum number of principles possible in any situation.

To illustrate the importance and constancy of principles, consider the U.S. economic troubles increasing in late 2007 and early 2008. To be sure, there were many innocent victims of circumstance but there were also many willing participants who chose to make decisions misaligned with principles. As of this writing, the widespread pain is being felt in our country and throughout the world. The point is not to judge others but to simply show consequences of principles hold steady regardless of how we may act or not. We dare not ignore these natural laws with their guaranteed outcomes. We can rant, complain or accept but these natural laws operate without our input. We can make choices but the consequences are determined by timeless principles.

Culture and Results

Why care about a model with which to view culture? Why care about culture for that matter? Despite what we may think about culture, it is present in any group, family, organization, state or country. Ignoring culture does not make it go away. Whining about cultural problems is no more useful. In short, whether we acknowledge it or not, culture determines output. It is as certain and death and taxes.

> **In short, whether we acknowledge it or not, culture determines output.**

If culture is a non-negotiable part of every enterprise in which we participate, it is logical to at least consider a passing interest in the topic. If the reader accepts this premise, then the model of *Expected End* is one viable theory for many human dealings and also gives us a way to make a positive difference in these dealings.

Just compare like businesses where one hums along with high morale and great efficiency and the other bumps along with petty employees and grumpy supervisors. The output of each group is likely to be decidedly different in both quantity and quality. It does not mean unhealthy cultures cannot produce; they do in spite of themselves. All cultures produce results of one type or another. The question then is what type of results do you want to produce? If you are satisfied with petty employees, cheap products, shoddy service, and low morale, do not work to change your current culture. If you think "just OK" is acceptable, do not waste time considering culture. If any type of result will do, then any cultural path will take you there and you can spend your time better on other issues. For everyone else who wants to improve employee morale, produce excellent products and services that fuel innovative solutions, work tirelessly on the culture. Culture makes an enormous difference.

Consider one consequence of culture: employee turnover. It does not take great intelligence to know turnover will be higher with a company of poor culture versus one with an excellent work climate. It just makes sense. We like to work at places we enjoy and it is sheer drudgery to put in time at the bad.

Now think of the service or product produced by a healthy culture. An employee who enjoys a place of employment will take more care in the process and turn out better widgets than the subordinate who keeps looking at the clock hoping for the end of the day. The same can be said for a service-based company.

Let's emphasize: culture always drives results. We ignore culture at our peril for consumers plainly have more selection in our era than ever before and are no longer captive to a business or agency simply because it hangs an "open" sign in the front window. More and more people are voting with their feet and you can be sure this decision is based on a cultural analysis even if called by a different name. A company can only thrive long-term if it gives sufficient attention to cultural issues. The bottom line is the leadership thinker must consider culture before results because culture produces the results.

A few years ago, I visited a brick-and-mortar store to buy a particular book. The sales clerk kindly informed me it would take two weeks to order and receive the book. I went home, ordered online and was reading the book within three days. Incidentally, the book store I visited went out of business less than a year after my visit so there must have been other dissatisfied customers as well.

The beauty of the linkage between culture and results is any self-serving organization can see financial benefits from creating great culture and outstanding output. Western consumers are increasingly impatient because they have more awareness of alternatives in every category. Every enterprise – whether for-profit or not, whether product or service based – has customers. Caring for the long-term success requires tuning into the internal culture to understand external customer behavior. The cultural explorer will likely learn a thing or two along the way about the internal customers as well. No organization is exempt from the internal and external effects of culture decisions.

> **Every enterprise – whether for-profit or not, whether product or service based – has customers.**

Key Points – Chapter 1

1. The culture model of *Expected End* always starts at "mindsets."
2. Find mindsets.
3. Develop theories based on the mindsets.
4. Put the theories into practice by moving to application.
5. Cultivate balance to help the organization sustain results.
6. Make all decisions based on timeless principles.
7. Culture matters because it determines the type and quality of output.

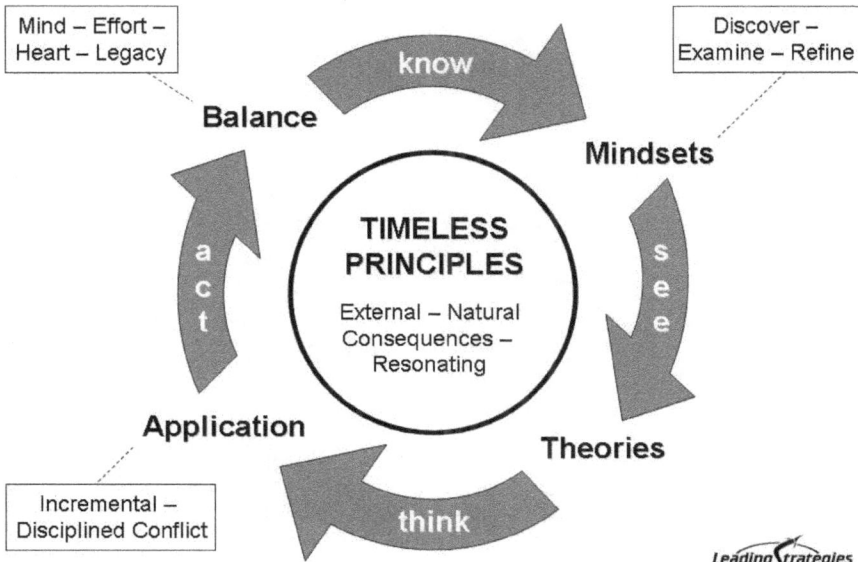

Expected End

Mindsets

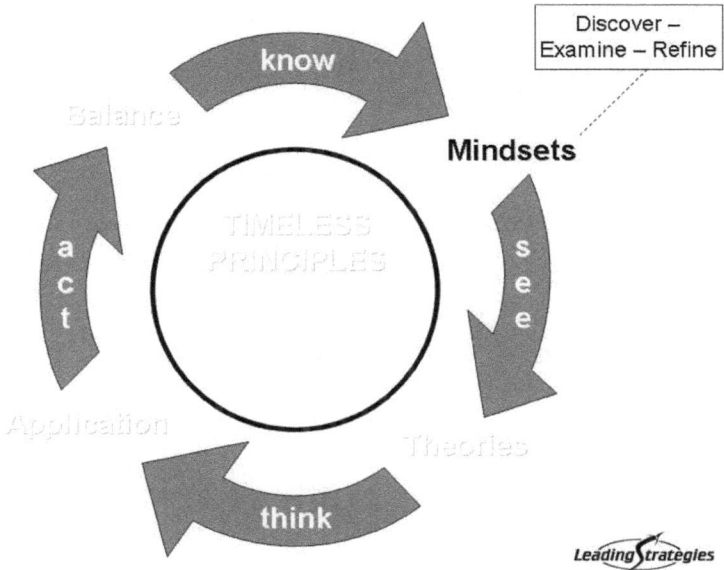

Chapter 2

The Path of Culture

"So, what do you see when you look at your children?" The question by the seminar speaker made a light bulb come on. I had been thinking about how to be a better Dad for my sons but was stuck. I had tried different techniques but was having inconsistent results. My boys were still quite young but I wanted to grow personally to better meet their needs. Now I realized improvement would not come from attempting new methods alone. Advancing depended directly on my ability to see in a broader, different way. Better methods would be driven by my mindsets.

The entry point in the *Expected End* model is always at "mindsets." How we see in a figurative sense is a crucial distinction that cannot be overemphasized for understanding and improving culture. Everyone has mindsets or paradigms. It is how we operate as people. Mindsets are also called paradigms mental maps, mental models, beliefs, assumptions or perceptions. Regardless of the phrase, this concept represents a mental way of seeing things.

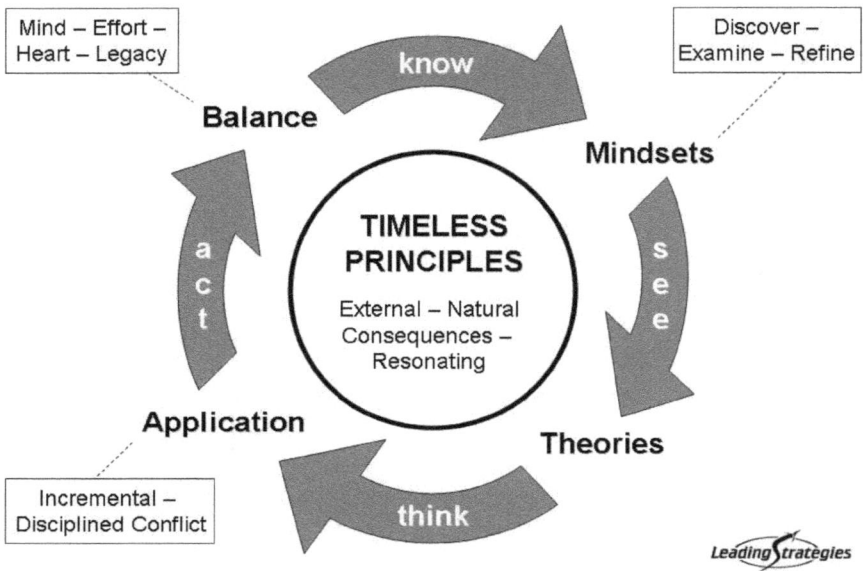

Before determining a solution to a problem, we must define the pieces of the issue. This becomes "how we see it" in a figurative sense. The labor of paradigm discovery is not for wimps as some discoveries are uncomfortable. However, pressing into this mindset examination also gives much helpful information and is the first step toward improvement. Now let's set the backdrop for considering culture in the first place.

Organizational Culture

What is culture? It is a collection of behaviors, an overall personality of a family, business or larger group of any size. Culture is present in any set of relationships whether it is two people or a major global corporation. How any collective unit behaves defines the culture and each grouping has its own innate values that determine action and responses. Each group also has sub-cultures with unique traits and preferences.

On one end of the spectrum is a climate dictating a certain set of very specific behaviors with all its related norms (such as the military). On the other end is a culture very loosely organized, fluid but distinct nonetheless.

Over history, we know cultural groups act and react differently than some or all of the individuals might behave alone. This is neither good nor bad of itself but important to remember when examining the culture. Leaders of many stripes have used this knowledge to their benefit and, in countless examples, to the benefit of a larger organization or movement.

The interplay of behavior in a culture is a most fascinating study and represents a stark display of critical mass. Any one individual is a complex blend of likes, dislikes, preferences, emotions, thoughts and values. One person may react in a variety of ways to the same issues depending on differences in the setting. Now multiply the large number of traits by the number of people in a group (with all their differences as well) and we have a dynamic

> **We know cultural groups act and react differently than some or all of the individuals might behave alone.**

persona that can rise to unexpected heights of greatness, flounder in mediocrity or inflict painful ill on its surroundings.

Real Life

The model of *Expected End* addresses real life because culture is very real and some would say too real at times. Culture impacts us at every turn and so we must choose whether to acknowledge this or operate with blinders and be a victim of circumstances.

While attending Air Force survival training, I saw in myself and others how the environment can make a difference. Personalities change and the revelations are not always pretty. Several of my classmates and I went to a restaurant on base for a regular meal after having virtually no sleep for 40 hours in a particularly difficult phase of the course. Upon having service slower than desired, I walked into the kitchen and rudely demanded our group be served more quickly. This was wildly out of character for me and I just hope they did not spit in the soup. Environment does have impact.

There were other examples too. While living off the land for a week in snow-packed Northern Washington, some team members who were once reliable turned into marginal help at best. There was even one in the group who required psychiatric help during some of the training activities. I do not say this critically considering some of the rigors of the training.

On the positive side, there were members who rose to the challenge of the circumstance and surprised the rest of us with their resilience and can-do attitudes. They pulled the weaker ones along and made good use of creative initiatives. This inspiring display reminded me there are some very incredible people among us and this is not always evident until the need is the greatest.

Sub-Culture

Every culture has sub-cultures within. In fact, there can be multiple layers to any culture depending on how perceptive the observer. Each family has unique individuals with their own "culture," each company has sub-units that behave somewhat differently than others. We are talking about cultures within cultures.

One of my first jobs of any length after high school was at a savings and loan and this was a first-hand introduction to corporate America. I spent the first two weeks at headquarters in a training environment. During this initial training, I met a co-worker who had started with the company in the mailroom. We will call him Justin and he had already formed a number of perspectives on the company. He knew who to contact to get an important project out of a bind to deliver results. Justin understood the personalities of headquarters, departments, branches and which departments tended to produce better than others. He knew which work areas were most helpful and he also knew about the company's sacred cows. Justin helped me start to understand both the overall cultural personality as well as the various sub-climates to better perform in this new environment.

Culture is Big

Some highly respected people have argued against looking at culture too much. They contend such an objective is far too ambitious and typically beyond the control of the average worker. They say culture is just too big. They argue what is really required is a strong and charismatic leader who occupies a position of great visibility. This person then can go on to lead the charge for improving culture. In other words, cultural concerns are only the domain of the powerful, positional leader. The rest of us had better get used to status quo.

The industrial age mindset made this true but the global outlook is moving into another phase of the information or knowledge worker. The model in this book assumes individuals can have an impact even if that input is small. One characteristic of the new knowledge worker generation will be a refusal to accept the word from one person on high to direct the ship unless there is solid reason for the order. Although unified action argues for a single person responsible for decisions, the continued flattening of organizations means more of the rank and file will have to think in deeper and more holistic ways than in the past. They will also need to be more forthcoming regarding input. Directorship will become less useful and leadership thinking will take its place.

It will be increasingly insufficient for the successful new worker to simply punch a time card at 7:59 AM, mindlessly stay busy through the day and then go home shortly after 5:00 PM. The changing cultural trend in the work world will demand a more flexible, clear-headed approach by more people to move any company in the direction demanded by customers.

There is no doubt impacting culture with any long-term effects is hard, especially for most of us who occupy a lower to medium level position. How do we gain a toehold to make the business more nimble? How is it possible for one person to make a difference? The simplistic answer is to first influence a sub-culture.

While this book does not pretend to give tidy answers to the searching questions by a student of culture, there are some common starting points to open an amazing vista. Keep in mind the first step in progress begins with awareness.

Culture Begins With Mindset

Awareness begins with exploring and understanding the concept of a mindset. Mindsets govern all we do as people as this is how we make decisions and is why the *Expected End* model starts with "mindsets." (Mindsets can also be called paradigms, governing perceptions, assumptions, mental maps, and a way of figurative eyesight.) All individuals and cultures have mindsets. For example, upon completing a transaction, we often hear a store clerk say, "Have a nice day." The person may or may not use this phrase outside of the store but there is a cultural mindset at work: "If we treat customers well, they will come back and buy more things."

If a company suddenly realized telling everyone to "have an awful day" would increase sales, some would do it. It goes right back to the mindset landscape. A company solely focused on making money to the exclusion of most or all other values will behave in such a fashion. This illustrates the presence of mindsets both individually and collectively all around and inside us.

Here are two less cynical examples. Most all of us have talked at one time or another with a school secretary. Just as in all professions, there are good ones and bad ones. What drives the behavior?

Let's consider the happy, helpful secretary. This person is a joy to be around and is liked by parents and children alike. There is no problem too difficult, no story too ridiculous. "Extra mile" is the watchword. For this person, the mindset may look something like, "If I am helpful to others, it will clear the way for better school performance."

On the other hand is the perpetually grouchy secretary. Dealing with this one is out of necessity and typically painful. Do not ask a question unless absolutely required is the rule of thumb here. The mindset of the secretary is probably along the lines of, "I am very busy and you are getting in the way of real work."

As U.S. fighter pilots, we constantly studied other aircraft of the world in order to have a working mindset on how best to fight. Different adversaries called for different strategies and tactics. Applying the wrong case study to an enemy would be disastrous and so we studied aircraft recognition as well. In our case, we knew this learning and re-learning could mean the difference between life and death so we had the ultimate incentive to excel. It was imperative to see each of the potential bad-guy airplanes as close to reality as possible. This was hard work at times as it required ascribing different attributes to other aircraft unlike our own.

> **Most companies look down on mediocre output. Ironically, neglecting serious mindset work guarantees cultural barrenness with equally mindless results.**

Although the potential outcomes in a business setting may not be nearly so grave, it is still incumbent on us to do the challenging work to understand our respective environments. Most companies look down on mediocre output. Ironically, neglecting serious mindset work guarantees cultural barrenness with equally mindless results. It is all too easy to ignore the mindset work and just pick a theory that is only a 30% solution. All such decisions have painful consequences.

Mindset Openness

In order to begin at the mindset stage in the model, it is essential to have mindset openness. This means an attitude of a learner that constantly evaluates other points of view based on eternal values or timeless principles (discussed in *Chapter 10*). An example of this openness occurred in the early part of my military flying career at Air Force Undergraduate Pilot Training (UPT – the initial 12-month school for training Air Force pilots.) During my time in the mid-1980s at UPT, the course was broken roughly into three parts. Graduates move on to advanced flying training and can take over two years to be certified as mission ready.

- Phase I – Orientation
- Phase II – Aircraft training (T-37 Tweet, a twin-engine, two-seat jet)
- Phase III – Aircraft training (T-38 Talon, a twin-engine, two-seat jet)

Upon beginning UPT, my classmates and I were open and eager to learn. We were like sponges to everything in the environment. When the base commander talked to us about how up to half of us would not graduate, our willingness to learn only grew stronger. When we heard war stories of how other students in classes ahead of us washed out, we were determined not to leave the course before graduation. We each thought and talked about the many questions churning inside of us.

"What makes the difference between a wannabe pilot and a UPT graduate? What will kill a UPT career? What are the most important things to know? How can we excel? Where do we start?" We were all about paradigm openness.

In an organizational sense, cultural change by its very nature requires openness to the environment. Here is a partial list of questions to ask about the organizational surroundings in order to define the ideal corporate mindset.

- What do the internal and external stakeholders want and need?
- Why does this matter to them? Why should we care?

- Which stakeholders are essential to our success? How far do we go in including their expectations? Should it vary by group?
- Which customers do we want to keep? Which clients will not be missed if they leave (in context of our purpose)?
- What are we passionate to deliver and where does this mesh with the stakeholder perspective?

The numbers in our UPT class slowly decreased and each loss was painful as the rest of us knew one of us could be next. One particularly difficult student to lose from the class had trouble learning to land the T-38. We will call him Mark. This was the second half of UPT so we all had become good friends. Even with extra flights and instruction, Mark could not get the picture on the higher landing speeds. He clearly had the aptitude to fly as he completed the first portion of UPT in great form. Landing the T-38 simply eluded him. He talked with the instructors and students, studied, practiced and still could not meet the standard. I suspect there was something Mark was not seeing as he had previously demonstrated an ability to fly very well. The rest of us were powerless to help so Mark eventually washed out. As I helplessly watched this event unfold, I was not aware of mindsets. Had I understood mindsets then, I would have had added tools to try and keep Mark in the game. How we see is critical to any other steps toward progress.

Paradigm Examinations

Stumbling onto a paradigm is one thing and critical examination is yet another. It is tempting at times when confronted with understanding a new paradigm to quickly move on without any more thought as some paradigms are not very pretty at first. The cultural student resists this natural urge to run away and plunges into the hard work of mindset examination.

Does it strike an emotional chord (positive or negative)? How complete is it? Does it accurately describe a set of assumptions that influence decisions? Who can help me analyze the new insight?

As a student pilot in the Air Force, one of the basic pieces in learning to navigate an aircraft on a low-level route was the clock-map-ground rule. Prior to the flight, we would mark a map with timing marks along the course. While flying, we would constantly check the clock, look at the map to determine where we should be and then look out the window to see where we actually were. If we did the process out of order, we would get into trouble.

For example, if I started by looking outside and then comparing to the map, I could talk myself into being several places on the map. This was a sure way to get lost. If I ignored the clock, I might be doing fine on the route but might not realize a shortage of fuel at the destination (to say nothing of the military expediency of reaching a target exactly on time). Examining perceptions is very similar in an organizational context. Resist the urge to move too fast around the model. Instead, work carefully and intentionally in finding and examining mindsets.

There are so many things we do almost unconsciously. Take something as simple as using a pencil, folding your arms or riding a bike. All these and many more actions are based on how we see the world. Once we have adapted to new mental territory, the paradigm becomes comfortable and then invisible if we let it. The student of culture will constantly foster better self-awareness and a team of students will do the same for a work group or organization. Part of self-awareness keeps as many mindsets as possible on the conscious level.

We can break mindsets into the categories of personal mental maps and group outlooks. Please realize the personal mental maps are essential building blocks to working on group outlooks.

Personal Mental Maps – A personal mindset is of one individual. The question is how close is the mindset to reality? Keep in mind the strongest-held mindsets are often invisible. Honesty in me regarding paradigms will determine what I see. Do I only see the hope side of the mindset or the reality side? Can I see both? Do I wish really hard that reality somehow matched my wishes? Not a good strategy. Am I willing to do the hard work to bump the hope against reality to advance in growth? Better approach.

Lacking recognition or consideration of mental maps will doom the theoretical leader to status-quo assumptions and make change and improvement impossible. The reason is if I cannot see what is at issue, there is no need to change. In this case, life is great without any alterations. If I can see a difference between hope and reality, honesty requires me to refine the overall mindset by choosing to accept or change the existing mindset. Therefore, in order to progress in personal improvement demands I must first personally see clearly before anything else can happen.

Group Outlooks – Just as individuals possess paradigms, so do groups, teams, departments, entire organizations and even countries. This is the larger-than-life backdrop where the leader must do the best work because mental maps control human behavior at all levels. The questions leading to discovery in the team and organizational awareness are quite similar to inquiries on the personal level. Start the sentence with "why" to discover a number of things. Sometimes, the findings are unpleasant but necessary all the same.

A fascinating project is to first list all organizational sacred cows or current practices considered untouchable. (Make sure to choose a safe environment and group for this exercise.) The newer people to your business are typically better at this because they have fresh eyes (i.e., mindsets). Now ask questions such as, why is this practice so hands-off? Why does it matter so much? What is the full history of the method? What timeless principles drove the original decision? Is the application of those principles still appropriate given our current setting, era and needs? Should the practice be updated or deleted? What will happen if we ignore the ironclad rule? What is the worst thing that can happen if we change? What is the best thing that can happen?

You may be surprised at the mindsets that pop up or the deafening silence of a paradigm vacuum. In other words, there once was a paradigm there but we do not know what it was or where it went. This sounds like it has morphed into blind action. Developing complete theory requires gaining and refining figurative eyesight plus a continual dissatisfaction with your current knowledge of it.

I once worked at a place where basic questioning was not allowed by previous supervisors. In the first group meeting, one of the members finally spoke up and said he just wanted me (the boss) to tell him what to do and he would do it. Others before me expected unquestioning compliance. This spoke volumes on the culture and the uphill battle we would have to inject health and openness into the conversations.

Test and Predict

I am not talented at golf but have been known to play from time to time for the social benefit. On one outing after I bludgeoned the little ball repeatedly through the first few holes, I noticed a small, older lady walking up to tee off on the first hole. She eyed the ball, paused for a moment and, with very conservative motions, hit the ball.

There was no large swiping sound or resounding whack. Instead, I heard just a little "tink." What was amazing was how the white ball sailed straight and far. I was dumbfounded and this proved to be a paradigm shift for me. Up to this point, I had focused mostly on the brawn approach to golf. I am still not great at golf but I often think of this one example when my knuckles get too white on the club handle. One hit by a senior citizen caused me to test and then change a paradigm.

Follow the "Mindset Map" below to test and change your paradigms. Step 1 is to simply observe some behavior. Step 2 is to ask "why, what and how" questions to determine the underlying mindset. Step 3 is the next natural progression that identifies at least one mindset. Steps 4 and 5 further refine the mindset by testing and modifying as needed. The validity of the mindset is determined by how well we can predict future outcomes based on the mindset. We will explore this further in *Chapter 4*.

Mindset Map

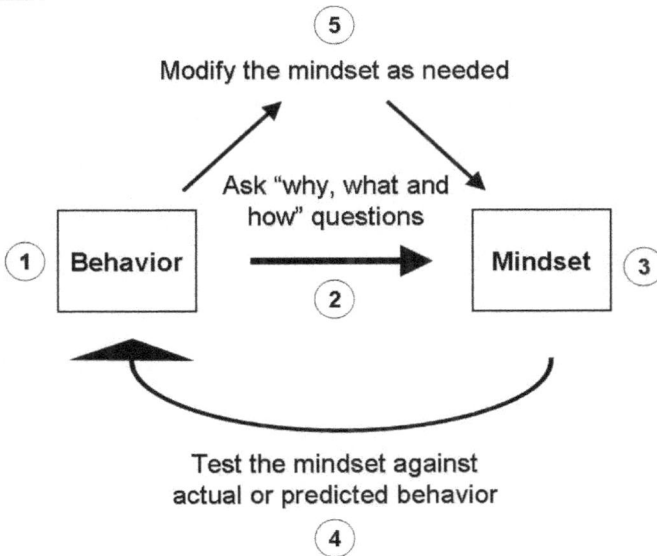

Mindset Impact

What if we leave out paradigm consideration altogether? Will the sky fall in? Not hardly. What will happen though, while more insidious, is just as serious. Thinking will only rise to the quality level of the current paradigm. If this mindset is significantly incomplete or otherwise lacks depth, expect the follow-on steps of the model (theory and application) to be shallow at best.

As a junior high student, I saved money and purchased an ant farm. It was an exciting moment to set everything up and watch the ants begin their remodeling work. It was a bit difficult to see parts of the colony because I had scratched the Plexiglas while loading the sand through the small hole at the top. It seemed silly that a manufacturer had made the hole so small for such a big job but I persevered and was proud of it. Imagine my embarrassment later when I realized the base could snap off in order to fill or refill the contents through a much larger opening. I had operated with an incomplete paradigm and the results were less than desired.

Fast forward to now. What are the potential human costs of us ignoring paradigm work? What great successes will never happen as a result? What innovations will remain unknown all because someone did not look hard enough for another mental map? What are the financial impacts of a better paradigm?

Key Points – Chapter 2

1. Culture is the personality of a group of any size.
2. Cultural behaviors vary with external pressures.
3. All cultures have sub-cultures.
4. Culture begins with a mindset.
5. Cultural change begins with mindset awareness and openness.
6. Find mindsets by asking "why, what and how" questions; predict and test results.

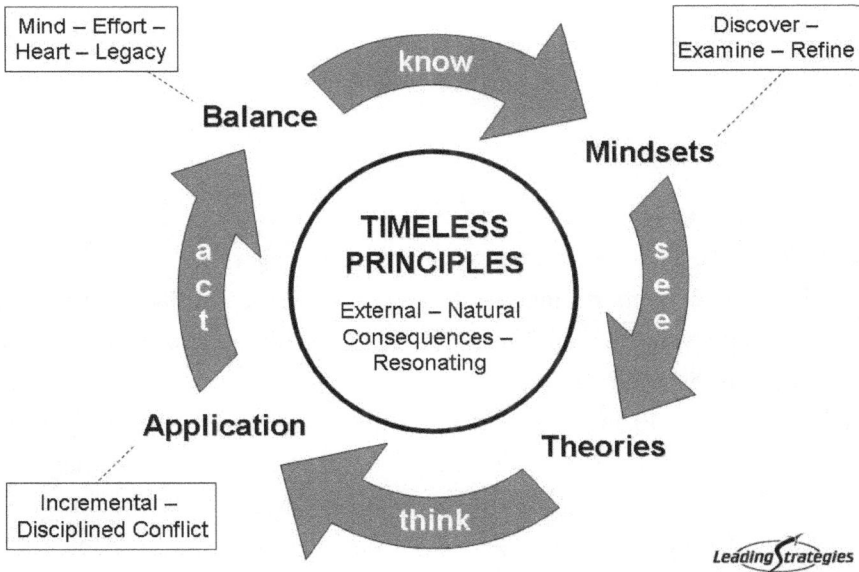

Chapter 3

So What Do You Think?
(and other sloppy questions)

"You were in the wrong place at the wrong time," the flight lead barked at me during the debriefing. I was painfully aware of my buffoonery but was frustrated over how to improve for the next time. We had gone out on what was to have been a routine training "Dart ride" mission in the F-4 Phantom II where we live-fired the 20mm gun against a towed airborne target. My brain fade this day was downright dangerous because of real bullets. As a new mission-ready pilot, I was still adjusting to flying with a group of very experienced but non-instructor type of pilots. Still, by any standard, this flight had not gone well for me.

We have all been there. A normally straight forward task goes sideways and there is no obvious explanation. Avoid the allure of finding a scapegoat to satiate the guilt. Start looking underneath the activity for understanding to begin the process of moving toward real solutions. Search deeper than the surface explanations. Question your questions because they also represent mindsets. Looking for, examining, understanding and modifying mindsets are all part of an essential first stop in working through the *Expected End* model.

One of the skills required of a fighter pilot is to predict geometry and fly accordingly. On the day of the Dart ride, I had calculated wrong and carefully maneuvered myself into a dangerous position in the swirl of airplanes. The debriefing after the flight did not help much as it was long on my failings and short on repair techniques. However, what happened next was very useful.

A veteran pilot took me aside and described what I had done, what I should have done, and, most importantly, why. His simple explanation

> **Question your questions because they also represent mindsets.**

made great sense and it worked on my next flight. Rather than being a hazard to the other airplanes twisting in the sky, I was an integral part of the team. The counsel of the more experienced pilot was great although it clashed with my earlier mindset. Presented with new information, I needed to make a decision on whether or not to change how I saw the issues. I chose the improvement course with great results.

The tips of paradigm icebergs can be ugly at times. It can become enticing to give up and work on something else. Persist. When there starts to be an emotional response, there is likely a learning point in the making. Emotional hints can cover the spectrum from anger to frustration to disappointment. (Some might call it passionately defending a point.) However you describe it, tune into the issue anytime you sense your heart rate pick up or realize you can speak easily from the heart on a matter. Although the initial sight of a previously hidden mental map may be frightening, additional exposure will almost assuredly enlighten rather than confuse.

A few years later in an F-15, I finished a training fight with a tracking gun kill on the opponent. This was considered a macho way to dispatch a bad guy and made the many hours leading up to the moment all worthwhile. On this day in the debriefing, another experienced pilot was very complimentary of my contribution to the mission. The encouragement I received from the other pilot in the flight was very gratifying. I had produced a great result while honoring expectations and took a few moments to enjoy the benefits of learning. The lesson I had learned several years earlier on an ill-fated Dart ride proved very helpful. I had new eyes.

Counsel versus Encouragement

A significant way to leverage mindset discovery is by seeking input from others. Outside perspective greatly helps clarify and develop our views on mindsets. We can divide seeking input into two categories: counsel and encouragement. There is a time and place for both.

Counsel will likely produce a collision of paradigms. If the hearers are open to improvement, the counsel is put to good use to examine current mindsets and adjust as needed. If good counsel is rejected, growth will not happen. Encouragement is an allied response or support for an initiative and is unlikely to challenge a mindset.

> **Counsel will likely produce a collision of paradigms.**

In most learning environments, the dialogue should be weighted to the counsel side but encouragement is needed as well. Each of us has some need to be recognized at least in some small way. Counsel can be the strong meat for improvement and encouragement can be the spice that makes the dish taste much better. It is possible to have the equation out of balance to either side.

This dynamic of using both counsel and encouragement in a wise manner aptly describes leadership thinking and creating high-performance cultures. Looking for genuine input and feedback is the mark of a committed cultural explorer. This trait of leadership is relatively easy to understand but much more challenging to do.

All Counsel and Nothing Else

One example of too much counsel for my experience level occurred while attending Fighter Lead-In Training at Holloman Air Force Base, New Mexico. I now wore the coveted wings of an Air Force Pilot and was looking forward to progressing in the study of combat flying. Some of my classmates departed UPT to fly air refueling tankers, others would pilot bombers, some would endure the curse of being a FAIP (First Assignment Instructor Pilot at UPT) and some of us would get to fly fighters. I felt extremely fortunate.

Within a few days of arrival, I was assigned a primary instructor with the call sign, "Crusher." At the time, I wondered if there was a story behind his call sign and it did not take long to find out.

This new phase of training focused on using the airplane as a weapon and not just flying from Point A to Point B. It was challenging and bewildering at first. It was not long into the first flight until Crusher's temperature started going up in the backseat of my AT-38. The smallest infraction would cause a loud outburst to further add to my newbie confusion. I was receiving counsel alright – blunt and unmistakable. If I would have had greater maturity, the guidance would have undoubtedly proved invaluable. However, I got mad instead.

After just two or three flights with the same pattern, I went to my flight commander (immediate boss) and petitioned for a new instructor. He was a patient, mellow man and listened carefully to my whining … uh … argument. Thankfully at the time, he overlooked my shallowness and complied with the request and I was relieved to get away from screaming Crusher. Ironically, I do not remember who the replacement instructor was and I probably lost a point or two from one of my buddies who started flying more with Crusher but that memory has mysteriously faded too.

Looking back, I wonder what I could have learned from Crusher had I been open to the counsel regardless of delivery style. Would I have become a better-rounded pilot? Would I have learned basic fighter maneuvers sooner and better? Would all the yelling have better prepared me for the rigors of flying fighters? Would the no-nonsense approach have made me a more aggressive fighter pilot? Probably yes to all.

Sloppy Questions

"So what do you think?"

"What are your thoughts?"

In most organizations, these questions (and other variations) require the hearer to make a decision: A) The asker wants my honest input so I will answer the question literally and truthfully, or B) The asker wants an ally so I had better make happy sounds. In many cases, the answer may be a guess depending on the people and matter involved.

We are still in the area of mindsets and a cultural influencer will try to be very explicit in questioning. If the intent of the questions above is clearly understood by all members, then they work fine. If not, beware to use more precise language. Do not ask, "What do you think" if you really mean, "Tell me again about the parts of my plan you like and pretend to like the rest." Do not ask, "What are your thoughts," if all you want is verbal support for your pet idea. You are not asking for another person's thoughts; you are asking for your own thoughts from another person's mouth. If that is your intent, fine. If not, say so. In any case, be clear about it. A big part of working through cultural diagnosis and prescriptions is about being real. Being real or not will make a huge difference in finding benefits from the *Expected End* model. More importantly, culture will not grow and improve with this sort of half-

> **You are not asking for another person's thoughts; you are asking for your own thoughts from another person's mouth.**

communication. Ultimately, the goal is to have shared definitions throughout so counsel and encouragement discussions happen in their rightful places.

Counsel AND Encouragement

A few years later, as an upgrading pilot moving from the F-4 to F-15, I had the privilege to fly with an instructor who found a great balance of counsel and encouragement. We will call him "Talon." He was exacting in his expectations with nothing soft about his standards but he also had a remarkably effective tactic. He consistently held me accountable for falling short of expectations while pointing out successes in the building block flights. This style fueled my motivation exponentially. It worked as well with my fellow students.

After each flight, Talon would talk through the chronology and point out areas for improvement and compliment those things that went well. He was very positive with me and recognized, as a driven, fighter pilot, my biggest fear was failure. After just a couple flights together, I was extremely committed to proving Talon's positive attitude right and I progressed smartly through the syllabus as a result.

At crucial points in military training, we test the bottom line of excellence by asking, "Am I willing to go into combat with this person?" The answer has a way of stripping any political correctness and speaks volumes. In the case of Talon, it would have been my honor to team up with him in combat. I hope it was mutual.

Here is the challenge. Peel away the feelings, self-serving motives and overly personal agendas and determine where you are on the counsel-to-encouragement continuum. Is the counsel truly aligned with the stated organizational vision, mission and values? (Notice I said "stated" because many companies say one thing and actually do another.) Be a blatant literalist for a moment and take the organization at its word. Is the encouragement fostering an environment to take the enterprise where it publically says it wants to go? If either or both counsel and encouragement are off track, what should you do?

Key Points – Chapter 3

1. Question your questions because they also represent mindsets.
2. Counsel seeks honest input and encouragement looks for reassurance; both are necessary.
3. Avoid sloppy questions without mutual definitions.
4. Strive to use both counsel (input) and encouragement (support).

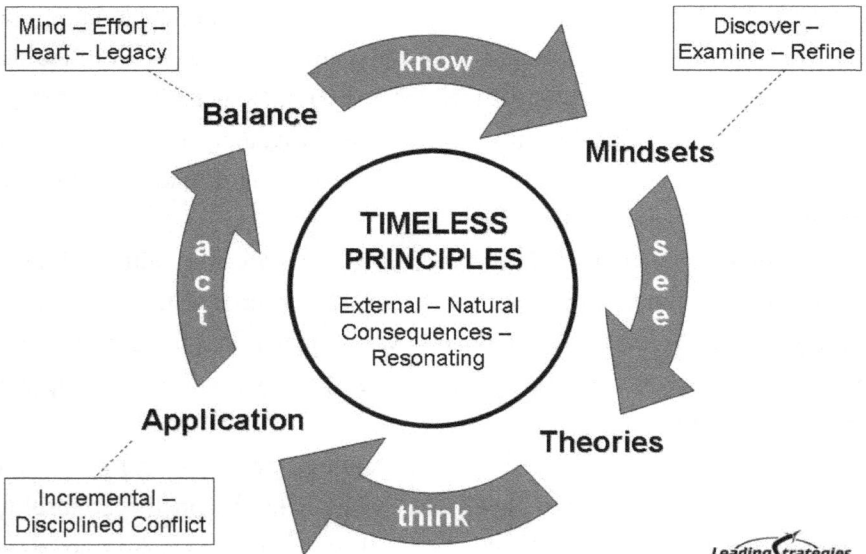

Mind – Effort – Heart – Legacy

Balance

know

Discover – Examine – Refine

Mindsets

act

TIMELESS PRINCIPLES

External – Natural Consequences – Resonating

see

Application

Incremental – Disciplined Conflict

think

Theories

Leading Strategies

Chapter 4

Diagnosing Mindsets

O ne of the best ways to discover mindsets is to start with a behavior and work backward. Many people have an easier time understanding the paradigm idea when it is linked to concrete action. Always carry plenty of humility on paradigm hunts because none of us can read minds with the possible exception of our own. We first discussed this idea of diagnosing mindsets in *Chapter 2*. The critical nature of this skill cannot be overstated as the theories and resulting application will only be as good as the paradigm definition. Use the "Mindset Map" below as a tool to help find reasonably accurate mindsets. This map works on both individual and group levels.

It is OK to start with small projects. Just start. Pick any practice or method (Step 1) and then explore its basis. This works on any level from the individual on up. Ask discovery questions of "why, what and how." (Step 2)

What drives this behavior? How did this practice come into being? What organizational need or value is satisfied by this method? Why do people consistently act this way in this environment? Do not be satisfied with the first few answers but keep digging until something resonates inside. Then and only then is there a chance of concluding on the underlying mental map controlling the behavior.

Mindset Map

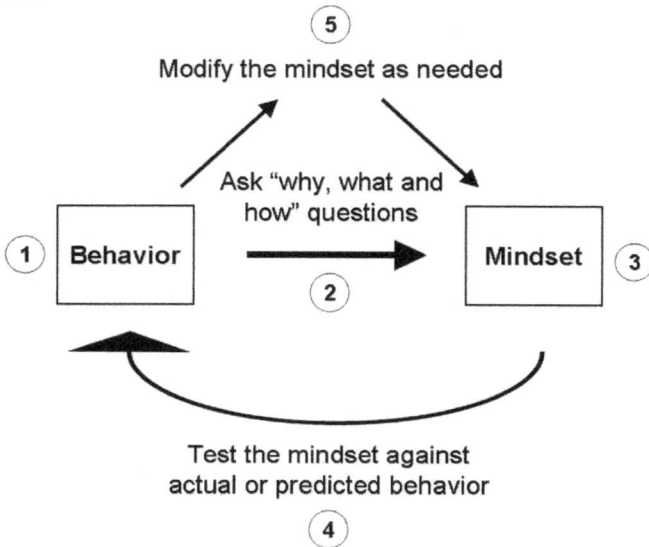

Upon defining a basic way of seeing (Step 3), test it out (Step 4). Can you accurately and consistently predict behavior based on this new knowledge? If so, you are gathering hard evidence to validate the mindset. Give the new assumption some "simmer time" to see if it lasts. Continue to test the mindset to see if it breaks down in any way. Are there behavior patterns that are different from the supposed mindset? Modify the mindset to better align with the behavior (Step 5).

To assist in the process, here are three hypothetical scenarios to illustrate how to understand mindsets. Do not focus as much on the specific questions as the intent for discovery. You may choose to add or delete steps based on your own style and experience.

Scenario 1 – Sam

Step 1 – Observed Behavior

- Sam is a good worker but is obnoxious at times with peers in his work area
- Sam works in an area with unique responsibilities requiring only one person

Step 2 – Why, What and How Questions

Q. Why are you sometimes obnoxious with your fellow team members? (Give specific examples of the behavior.)

A. Sometimes they are too slow about getting their work done.

Q. What bothers you about their slowness?

A. They are not working hard enough to pull their own weight in this office.

Q. How does their not pulling their own weight impact you?

A. It's not fair that I work so hard and they do not.

Q. What would fairness look like?

A. For one thing, they should not talk as much while working because it distracts me.

Q. Why do you sometimes engage in extended conversations in the work area?

A. I only talk for any length of time on important issues.

Step 3 – Mindset

- Sam wishes to be the boss and does not have a mature sense of teamwork

Step 4 – Test the mindset against actual or predicted behavior

- Is Sam willing to take on a project as the lead? Will he take responsibility for the outcome?
- Does Sam's ability to work on a team depend on the personalities involved?

Step 5 – Modify the mindset as needed

Scenario 2 – Human Resources Department

Step 1 – Observed Behavior

- HR always does a mad dash clean-up when the big boss is scheduled to visit
- HR is extra friendly to the big boss and laughs at all his/her dumb jokes

Step 2 – Why, What and How Questions

Q. Why is the HR area the cleanest when the big boss is scheduled to walk through?

A. We want the big boss to have less to pick on when he is here.

Q. What sorts of things does the big boss pick on besides the tidiness or lack thereof of the work area?

A. Sometimes, he will start to look more closely at some of our paperwork because he used to work in HR a long-time ago. Some of his regulatory knowledge is outdated.

Q. Why do you laugh at his jokes that seem so stupid?

A. I am just laughing with other people.

Q. Why do other people laugh at the dumb jokes?

A. We want to be polite.

Q. Why are good manners important with the boss?

A. He has a big say in my career.

Step 3 – Mindset

- People in this department are afraid of the big boss
- If HR looks really good, the big boss will not spend too much time visiting so the members can get back to work reasonably soon.

Step 4 – Test the mindset against actual or predicted behavior

- Watch the faces and body language of the HR members next time the boss shows up. What emotions can you detect just under the surface?

- Are there any signs of fear?
- Is there a sense of hurrying the boss along to his next appointment?

Step 5 – Modify the mindset as needed

Scenario 3 – ABC Services, Inc.

Step 1 – Observed Behavior

- Employees are irritated when a customer asks one question too many
- Employees have trouble answering more than basic questions

Step 2 – Why, What and How Questions

Q. Why are you so easily irritated by customer inquiries?

A. They are so annoying.

Q. What do you find annoying about the questions?

A. The questions are often the same.

Q. Why is this bad?

A. I have so many other things to do.

Q. Such as …?

A. Stocking shelves, updating inventory files and building displays.

Q. How do you determine the priorities for your day?

A. My boss tells me what is important.

Q. What are the typical priorities for the day as set by the boss?

A. Keep the shelves stocked and always present a neat appearance.

Q. What advice does your boss give regarding customers?

A. All in-store advertisements and products are displayed very clearly and already give sufficient information for most customer questions.

Step 3 – Mindset

- My boss sets my daily priorities and stocking shelves is a higher priority than answering customer questions.
- Employees have a greater responsibility to please the boss than the customer.

Step 4 – Test the mindset against actual or predicted behavior
- Are shelves stocked most of the time?
- How often does an employee answer more than one question from the same customer without showing mild irritation?
- How often does the employee tell a customer "It is on aisle 7" versus offering to take the customer there?

Step 5 – Modify the mindset as needed

Exercise

Now you try it. Take any observed behavior and then work back to the paradigm. This may be easiest at first with your young child or spouse. The most important factor is to pursue understanding based on good conscience and a desire to improve the organization, not tear down people. If the conversation becomes overly emotional, you will be wise to pause until another time to avoid damaging relationships. CAUTION: Please be very careful as this exercise is focused on diagnosis not blaming or criticizing.

Ground Rules
- Focus on issues, not people (personally).
- Listen with the heart to understand a whole message.
- Be very open to new perceptions, assumptions and theories.
- In part, people are products of their environments so give them consideration for this.

Step 1 – What is the behavior?

Exercise, continued

Step 2 – Raise the behavior with the people in a way that does not focus on them personally. The best technique is to talk with the group members one-on-one. Ask "why, what and how" questions with humility and focus on the whole message. Just go wherever the dialogue takes you without preconceived notions while keeping an eye on genuine discovery.

Step 3 – Determine one or more mindsets to account for the behavior.

Step 4 – Test the mindset against past behavior and then predict future behavior based on the new information. Observe behavior and see if it matches the prediction.

Step 5 – Modify the mindset as needed based on the observed behavior.

Key Points – Chapter 4

1. Identify a practice or method.
2. Ask discovery questions to determine the underlying mindset.
3. Rigorously compare the mindset against actual or predicted behavior.
4. Modify the mindset understanding as needed.

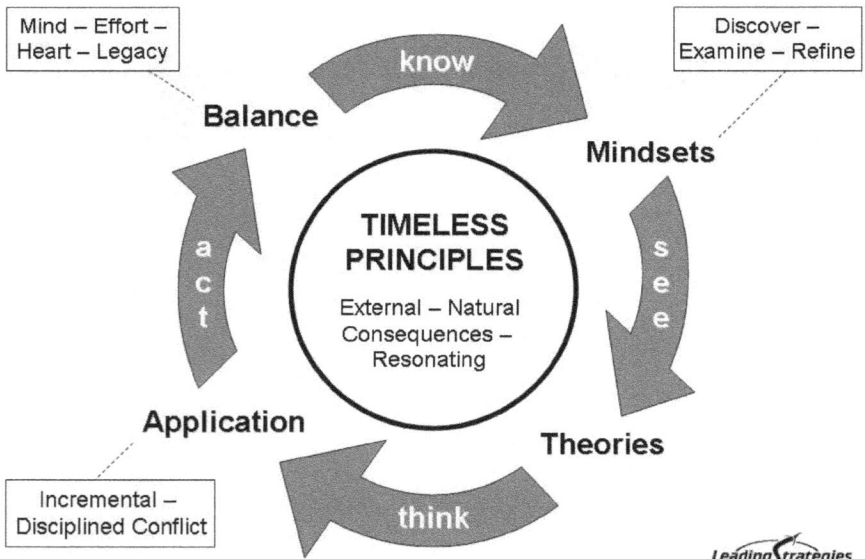

Expected End

Theories

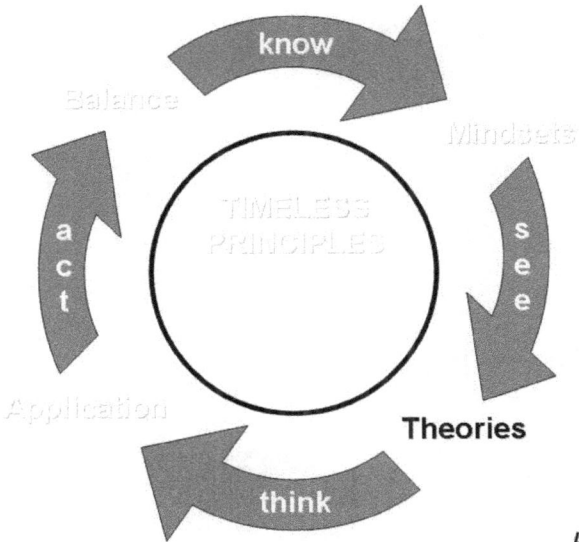

Chapter 5

Build a Bridge

Progressing to better cultural understanding requires moving from just looking at mindsets to developing theories based on these mindsets. Since culture always drives results, theories created from clear-headed mindsets are integral in this process. We previously looked at the various pieces of discovering, examining and changing mindsets to build a sufficient foundation. Now that we have what we think is a decent working mindset, what is next? The answer is to build a bridge of theories spanning the gap between mindsets and application. Here is the first example.

It all started with an idea. (An idea is a theory until it moves into execution or application.) More than one resource manager voiced a concern about the lack of training in managing unit finances. As Budget Director, I could see there was a problem from our end as well given the spotty and large variation in unit budget execution. There had been finance training in the past but it was time to create an update due to changing systems, regulations and methods. The first step was to realize there was an issue. The second challenge was to now build a useful curriculum.

As I talked more with the different managers, some were eager to assist in forming a solution for the larger set of needs. In a short time, I asked a cross-section of these resource managers to serve on a temporary working group to set up appropriate training. We discussed the needs and expectations of a variety of stakeholders including new or experienced managers and the finance office requirements as well. As we brainstormed and strategized, our theory quickly developed into a creative approach.

Over the next several months, we worked and re-worked both the training tools and methods and eventually presented the package to the entire group of 24 resource advisors. Their responses were very positive as they had actively participated in the solution.

Plan Ahead

Here is another example of a working theory that forms a bridge between a mindset and application. As a student in UPT, one of the skills we developed, particularly in the T-38 phase, was planning while performing aerobatics. The T-38 is fast and burns lots of fuel in a short time. Consequently, the instructors harped on us to string aerobatic maneuvers together without delays. This required constant attention to our location in the working area quickly followed by considering and choosing the next maneuver. We had to constantly work toward the center of the area, completing as many aerobatic maneuvers as fuel allowed.

> **Theories bridge mindsets and application.**

Theories are an essential bridge between seeing the landscape (mindset) and actually doing something (application). Theories bridge mindsets and application. If we see a problem but neglect the hard work of developing a plan, what is the point of understanding the issue? If we jump to just do something without a theory, the chances for failure are very high and, worse yet, we will not learn because there is no standard upon which to measure. There is no comparable so the action is in a vacuum. We might describe this as "action by bewilderment" and it is not terribly effective.

In the military environment, we worked to have theories on every conceivable contingency in order to be as prepared as possible. In a threat environment, crisis is normal and while there cannot always be a script, a partially developed theory will do just fine. At times, the mental preparation alone was useful even if the theory did not quite work as advertised. There is a benefit even in an incomplete process if the intent is genuine.

It is valuable to continually assess the paradigms and develop theories accordingly. We never reach perfection and so continual attention to this area benefits the individual, group or team. The more we work theories, the more we discuss and evaluate the underlying paradigms. This in turn leads to better understanding of the mindsets at play which also allows for better theories. It works well together.

In real life, theories and mindsets are tied together. It is most effective to understand the individual distinctions between the two concepts while recognizing the ever present link between them. Remember, a mindset is how we see the environment and the theory is a way to deal with what we see. As we build theories, invariably there will be questions that trace immediately back to the underlying mindset. Not only is this necessary to adequately uncover the mindset but is a way to test the theory based on what we think the paradigm may be.

> **A mindset is how we see the environment and the theory is a way to deal with what we see.**

One of the initial skills to develop as a student of culture is theory-building. The more theories per mindset, the better as this will only serve to expand the questions that measure, validate or disprove the mindset. This is really just brainstorming with each possibility a bit more involved than a single option.

Sharp Thinkers

The mind is incredibly powerful. The question though is how well do we use our thinking capacity? On the road from mindsets to theories, pushing our mental abilities as far as possible will not map the available space out there. There is far too much geography. The intent here is not to push philosophy for its own sake but as a vital stop on the way to incredible culture. The better the early work in forming coherent theories the finer the results will be. Keep in mind, there is a constant dynamic between all the elements of the *Expected End* model in the pursuit of extraordinary cultures. Those who will search for valid mindsets and then work hard to form reasonable theories are what we will call "sharp thinkers." You will notice the "think" arrow in the model diagram below is what gives legs to a theory to move it around the model.

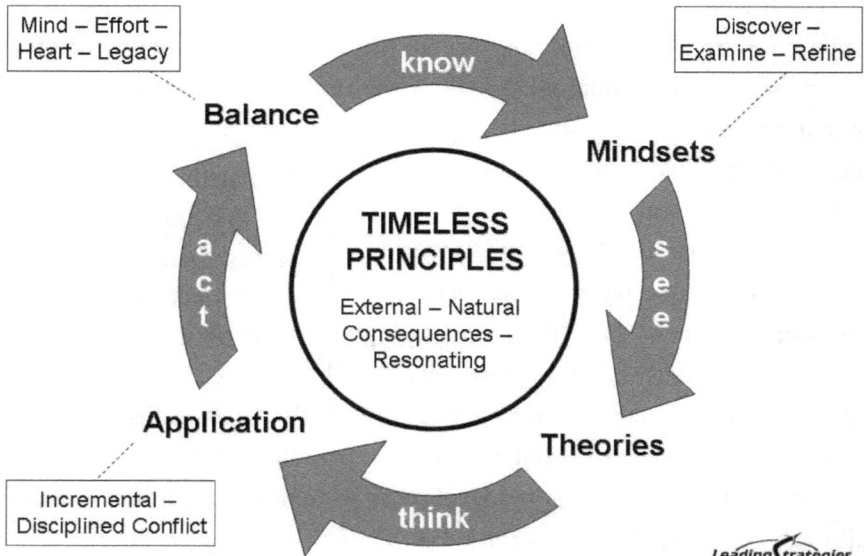

We are really good at working *in* systems but we need to become much better at working *on* systems as well. Sharp thinking is a much higher than average standard of deliberating. Sharp thinking is not critical in the sense of tearing down but it is relentless in focusing the thoughts and underlying assumptions.

It is so easy to just go along and accept what has been handed down and comfortably work in the status quo. After all, most of us are very busy with family, work, the extracurricular and life in general and could easily pass by creating new theories based on our mindsets. To spend added time in forming theories takes discipline and mental work but is necessary in order to release pent-up creativity.

If more of us would engage in this experimentation-of-ideas practice even in a small way, the influence would be impressive. We are talking about committing to cultural excellence initiatives to transform organizations of any size. Such healthy, principle-based environments spawn unbridled innovation followed by great results. The more we exercise the awareness of mindsets followed by theory development muscles, the stronger the outcomes will be. Please take a moment to review the characteristics of Sharp Thinkers listed below.

Characteristics of Sharp Thinkers

- Foster curiosity in themselves
- Cultivate great questions
- Maintain the highest standard of self-awareness
- Reinforce personal humility continually

Foster Curiosity

It is natural to be born with curiosity. How many of us had to "baby-proof" our homes for either our own or other's children all because of mobile curiosity. Somewhere in our growing up years, curiosity can fade to where we stop learning as deeply or enjoyably. In fact, there are many organizational environments where curiosity will put you in hot water faster than most other traits.

Curiosity is fun and will fuel an endless supply of searching questions. Throw off the chains of unimaginative thought and wonder about possibilities just like a child. This does not discard previous learning but builds upon it. Combining current knowledge and experience with healthy curiosity produces amazing leverage.

Curiosity grants permission to ask things that may appear silly to the casual observer but are really quite insightful. You can even say, "This might be a dumb question but I am curious ..." See, curiosity gave you a pass. In the process of cultural improvement, curiosity is a great friend. Curiosity is the fuel for any cultural improvement initiatives because without it, change efforts will not go the distance once their romance loses its luster. Cultivating a curious environment is a necessary part of improving culture.

Cultivate Great Questions

I once worked with a lady who exhibited several sharp thinking attributes. Sarah's inquisitive mind would not let loose of a topic even if our group struggled to form a reasonable theory. She easily questioned paradigms to further refine the notional solutions and was persistent in finding better understanding.

In one conversation, Sarah asked a very senior member of our organization a blunt question regarding his future plans for our business. She did so in a respectful way but there was no mistaking her desire to learn and engage. It was obvious she had a working mindset and theory. On that memorable day, Sarah hit a home run with her questions and the senior executive could not so much as find his baseball mitt. Sarah's inquisitive nature and fearless way of asking questions continue to inspire me today. We can never become too good at asking great questions.

Since we are talking about sharp thinking, use the great questions to influence others. You likely have more sway than you may think. At one point in my military career, a Commander decided he would like the finance office to move to another building. He had a list of good reasons and so it looked like it would happen.

My staff came to me and argued from an operational standpoint why we should stay put so I took this to the Commander. Frankly, I was pessimistic we would prevail. But surprise, surprise, a series of conversations over a few weeks saw the initiative die and we stayed in the office that better met the spectrum of needs. Never underestimate the power of a few well-placed questions. Do not be obnoxious about it; just do the right thing at the right time.

Cultivate Self-Awareness

In our busy societies, it is all too easy to let ourselves off the hook for the challenging mental work of culture change. It is much like trying to complete a project with the wrong tools. My family and I were once stranded with car trouble all because we did not have the right tool to remove a 10 cent fuse. Neither my wife nor I could quite get our fingers on the offending part and we fussed with the problem for about 30 minutes before deciding to borrow a pair of needle-nose pliers. It took longer to find a set of pliers than it did to replace the fuse. In no time, we were on our way.

Having the right tools makes all the difference. One of the tools for the cultural influencer is self-awareness. In our context, self-awareness means understanding the likely personal responses to anything in our environment. Growing in personal understanding requires an attitude of learning and accountability. In not holding ourselves accountable to find paradigms and develop appropriate and related theories, we are like someone trying to walk through sticky glue and this will stunt growth in self-awareness. The unwillingness to be self-accountable is much like laboring with the wrong tools for a job and requires extra effort to make precious little progress. Sharp thinkers hold themselves accountable.

Reinforce Humility

The humble have realistic perspective on their station in life regardless of position. Humility is closely tied to self-awareness and is the recognition of the potential knowledge, skills and abilities available compared to the small amount possessed. Success can be the antitheses of humility for the weak-minded but the greatest people never lose sight of how much better they can be in the future and still never reach perfection.

To be humble is to be open, teachable and willing to offer honest thoughts in return. This attitude of humility connects a deep personal satisfaction with a relentless desire to improve. Take a humble approach everywhere and watch your cultural influence grow. We will cover humility in more depth in *Chapter 10*.

Key Points – Chapter 5
1. Theories bridge the gap between mindsets and application.
2. Plan ahead based on intentional mindsets.
3. Sharp thinkers are those who will persist in finding valid mindsets and developing reasonable theories based on these mindsets.
4. Sharp thinkers are curious, ask great questions, hold themselves accountable and cultivate humility.

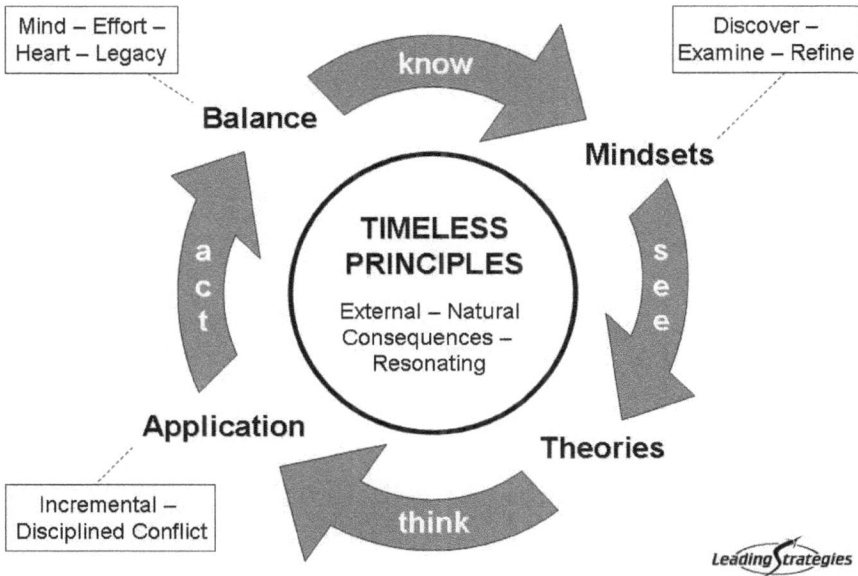

Expected End

Application

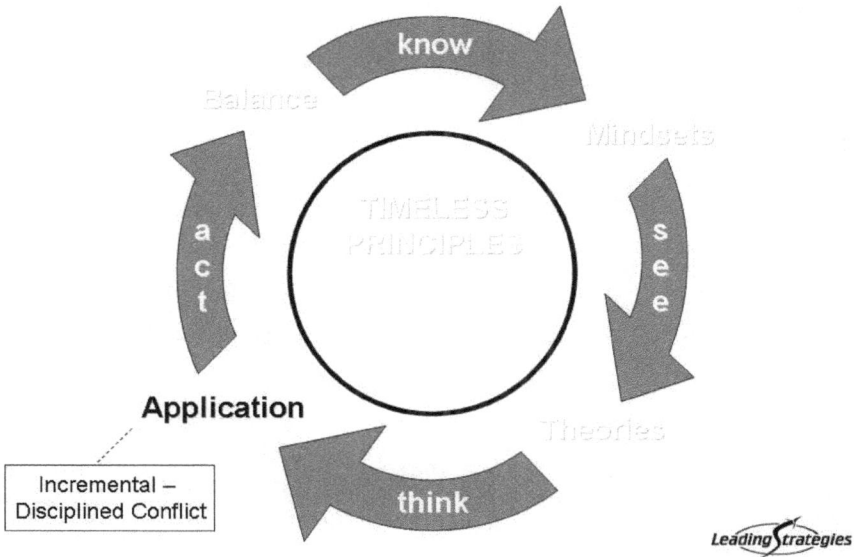

know

Balance

Mindsets

act

TIMELESS PRINCIPLES

s e e

a c t

Application

Theories

Incremental –
Disciplined Conflict

think

Leading Strategies

Chapter 6

Looking for Results

Application can be a tremendously intimidating prospect but it is the third and necessary stop in the *Expected End* model. *Chapters 6* and *7* explore application. Moving to application can challenge the student much like easily hearing an instructor's explanation in class only to be completely confused later by the homework assignment. Here are some application thoughts for the cultural explorer wanting to change into a cultural influencer.

- Review the *mindsets* on the issue at hand. How do you see it? What limitations can you find with your assumptions? Does the paradigm still look valid? Check with others to find out how they see the underlying definitions.

- Check the *theories* on how to address the mental map. Have you covered most or all of the mindsets and does this seem to bridge the gap between mindsets and application? What are the potential pros and cons of the outcomes? Again, what do others say? How will their perspectives shape your assumptions?

- Move to *application*. Do not spend too much time planning when in reality it is important to both think and then act. How flexible are you in adjusting to the real environment? Can you make changes on the fly to improve application?

- Evaluate the *application* through disciplined conflict. Once the task is completed, how did it go? Of the less-than-stellar parts, how did the mindsets and theories impact this result? What surprises popped up? Again, how did the mindsets and theories affect the outcome?

> **Resist the urge to treat a symptom without a clear understanding of what is driving the behavior.**

Quit Talking and Start Doing

I will always remember my first T-37 formation flight. Up to this point in training, being close to another airplane in flight was always bad and so I spent most of this particular flight worrying about not running into my buddy's airplane. We took turns flying the lead and wing (follower) positions and, in hindsight, our flight instructors must have had nerves of steel.

Flying so close to another airplane was the beginning of a firsthand experience in a theory on mutual support between two or more aircraft. As with most endeavors, this new skill looked fairly straightforward on paper and in the briefing room. The application was not quite so neat and clean. This fundamental building block for flying combat was vital to our progression as professional combat pilots.

To be effective, it is necessary to think well *and* do well. Application is the true test of all the ideal scenarios. The student in search of a better corporate climate must try things. The healthier the culture, the more people will try and this is all the more beneficial to the organization. In other words, the beneficial practices build on themselves because the safer it is to experiment, the more it will happen. This creates positive momentum and is a high-leverage activity to build a climate for change.

To assist the cultural student, *Expected End* application can be developed in bite-sized pieces. Start with smaller parts of a larger issue. For example, if you want to change customer service from a department into a core value, first make a list of behaviors that define customer service. Next, choose one of these parts and work on it alone. Maybe it is something simple like people answering and talking on the telephone in a more pleasant way. Work through the mindset and theory process and then start consulting with others on how to improve the paradigm and resulting theory for better application. As you make gains on the first piece, add other parts to the mix. Be sure to watch out for unintended consequences that may impact the larger issue or company.

Formal / Informal Communication

In order to move forward in application, communication is an essential ingredient that cannot be overdone. In turn, part of trust rests in communication. It can be surprising how we are perceived by others. I might think I am efficient and business-minded while another person might say I am short-tempered and inconsiderate. A true culture influencer is very interested in growing in self-awareness to improve communication and thereby cultivate high-trust relationships. Of the number of bosses I have worked for over the years, a few stand out as the ones for which I would still drop everything and go help with a moment's notice.

One afternoon while working on a vexing issue in my office, my boss showed up and asked if there was anything I needed from him. This type of question can be taken at least two ways. The first possibility is the boss cannot wait to jump into the fray and be Mr. Fixit. A second option is a supervisor who is genuinely interested in removing any obstacles for the good of the team. In this case, my boss was in line with the second type. I had grown to understand he really did want to help and he stayed engaged with the challenges we were experiencing without micromanaging our processes. He merely expected us to remain aligned with vision, mission and values and ask for assistance when needed. On this particular day, all I needed from the boss was that he was willing to be available if necessary.

In every organization, there are the formal and informal communication networks. An effective cultural leader needs to be aware and skilled at both. At first, most people will find a natural comfort level with either formal or informal communication but not both. Great communication must be multi-faceted so the culture changer will work to become proficient in both formal and informal communication environments and promote the free exchange of ideas so needed in cultural movements. A sharp thinker will cultivate the formal and informal systems as needed to serve principled ends. It is important to emphasize principled ends as many an unethical or corrupt boss has misused communication channels. The crucial measure is whether or not the method is for the long-term good of the organization versus self-serving for the individual superior or senior team.

Listening

Perhaps one of the most difficult components of communication for many is listening. It is challenging to listen in only a receive mode where all the speaker is doing, saying, feeling, and thinking is studiously absorbed. Listening is another important part of application because feedback must become as close to effortless as possible for improvement to happen in the culture. This is a pivot point. Since over half the message arrives in the form of non-verbal cues, accurate meaning requires a carefully honed set of full senses. It is very incomplete to simply hear the words and ascribe dictionary meaning. How are the words relating to subtle visual cues? Does the sender's body language seem to emphasize, agree or disagree with the words? What is implied, not said? What is the emotional temperature? A fascinating point is how well most people can naturally read the whole meaning if they focus sufficiently on the sender. So often, a lot of us tend to be in a hurry and miss subtle clues in a conversation.

In order to have high awareness of organizational mindsets and the work environment, the would-be influencer of culture must constantly engage in the high-stakes game of communication. This is real work and without purposeful effort, there is much missed potential.

One of the ways to practice this is to become a better listener when not directly in a conversation. For example, while hosting a conference, roam about during small group exercises and really tune into each speaker. What are they trying to say? What are the subtle meanings? What are the important things unsaid? How many and what type of emotions are in the exchange? What do you perceive in body language (do not over-think it – just take in the many messages).

> **Listen as much or more with your eyes as with your ears.**

Another way to practice listening skills is to observe others during a presentation. How are they responding to the speaker? What points are resonating and what parts are putting them to sleep? What subtle emotional cues do you see? Listen as much or more with your eyes as with your ears. If one or more senses are physically debilitated, sharpen the remaining senses to take in as much data as possible in order to ascribe real meaning. By improving in listening, communication awareness will increase to new heights.

Simpler yet, practice observation in any conversation to pick more than the average number of data points from not only the person speaking but the other listeners as well. How do you perceive each person's processing? Who is engaged in the conversation and who is bored? Do you have any theories as to the "why"? It is difficult to find someone too good at listening. Use this continual stream of information to moderate your speaking. Speak to the emotions as well as the conversation content. These are all elements of improving the expected end.

Key Points – Chapter 6
1. Move into application with an incremental or step-by-step approach (crawl, walk, run).
2. Application requires great communication and this cannot be overdone.
3. Great communication requires great listening.

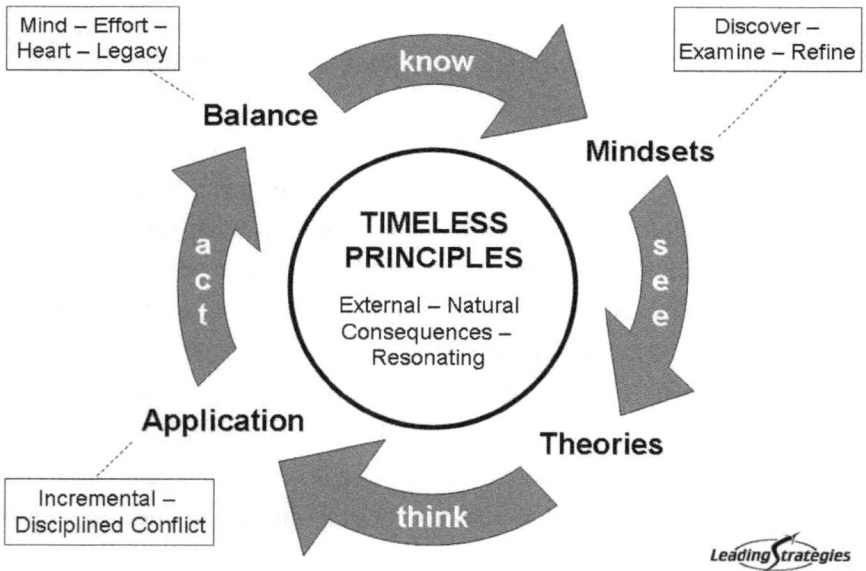

Chapter 7

The Conflict Advantage

"If your boss demands loyalty, give him integrity. If your boss demands integrity, give him loyalty." John Boyd

Conflict is common to the fighter pilot world. There is the natural clash of using aircraft as weapons against enemies. There is the paradox of a competition of egos combined with a high level of teamwork very similar to some professional sports settings. There is also a consistent environment of disciplined conflict among the aviators.

A cultural movement can only flourish with disciplined conflict. Without the honest exchange of ideas and the consequence of better mindsets and theories, cultural improvement is a pipe dream. The trick is to channel the conflict into useful means as it can harm the organization and the people in it if used incorrectly. You could compare this to using any dangerous piece of equipment. In the hands of a skilled worker, the tool is an awesome thing; used carelessly or for the wrong job, the same piece of machinery will create a disaster.

Before each flight in the fighter pilot world, the participants go through a predictable routine of mission planning and briefing running the gamut from checking the weather and airfield conditions to talking about the specific tactics for the flight (briefing). The pilot in charge or flight lead methodically works through the flight from the moment of engine start-up to shutdown. The flight lead clearly presents the expectations in an organized manner.

After the flight, the aviators meet to talk about what happened in order to improve for the future (debriefing). Again, the flight lead walks through the flight from start to finish but this time, the flight members are expected to give much more of their individual thoughts and perspectives. Sometimes we would joke it was one thing to win an engagement in the air and quite another to win the debriefing. Sometimes the pilot with the greatest advantage in the debriefing was the one holding the white board markers.

> **The better a culture becomes at disciplined conflict, the better the cultural health will be.**

One of the core values of the fighter pilot world is giving unvarnished views on any discussion of strategy, tactics, and general flight assessment; it is a matter of life and death in peacetime and wartime. In an organizational setting, the seriousness is not as obvious but there are real costs just the same. Failing to give open input will ultimately degrade a product or service. What customers will be impacted by this? Who may never become a customer because we failed at having a principled exchange of internal ideas?

Despite the sometimes harsh setting of blunt feedback, the discussions in the fighter pilot environment were conducted with much discipline. Because we are talking about people, there were times when tempers wore thin. Yes, there were shouting matches and injured egos at times but the overall theme was disagreement in a measured way.

The better a culture becomes at disciplined conflict, the better the cultural health will be. This is what true communication is like and, as we discussed in the last chapter, great communication is required to move into the application part of our model. There must be an open exchange of ideas that respects the participants. Show me a culture where everybody agrees all the time and I will show you a group where the majority is asleep, numb or swallowing their tongues. This idea of regulated disagreement focuses on issues, not people. It takes a high level of maturity to not allow the exchanges to fall into emotional overload with little progress but it is possible.

Disagreement and Disrespect

Discovery is an amazing part of the leadership journey. The ability to discover is based on the skill of searching for and examining personal paradigms or mindsets. In the story by Hans Christian Andersen, *The Emperor's New Clothes*, a foolish ruler parades naked through his kingdom after neither his court officers nor he will admit a set of clothes are only imaginary. It is a relief when an honest child puts an end to the nonsense by telling the truth about the emperor's lack of clothes. (Andersen, 2004) The lesson of this children's story can be applied to the organizational environment.

For our context of seeing and improving culture, I will speculate the emperor cultivated an environment of fear where contributing open thoughts was not allowed and perhaps severely career-limiting. How else can we explain the lack of input from the Chamberlin and Treasurer after they review the non-existent clothes? The king had made a decree to have the new clothes so there was no turning back, no re-visiting an edict. Certainly, these court officials also had pride as they wanted to appear intelligent. However, we could speculate this pride was a result of how the boss (emperor) expected others to always have the right answers and not look stupid. The easiest way to look smart in many organizations is to simply follow the boss's lead and support all initiatives no matter how questionable they may be. A dysfunctional culture will reward this type of behavior; a healthy culture will not.

It is natural to like our own ideas best. Most of us do. The mistake comes, when we fall in love so much with an idea as to equate any disagreement with personal disrespect. This is a danger all would-be leaders must guard against to allow the free flow of ideas from those who care about an organization. Disagreement is not the same as disrespect. These are two distinctly different concepts. Certainly, it is possible to disagree and do so with disrespect and this is acted out with insults, overly sarcastic language, exaggerated disgust with another person, and so on. On the other hand, it is possible to disagree and be respectful at the same time.

> **If we all agree too easily, too often, we either have the wrong people on the team, are in serious need of cultural reform or both.**

For instance, when a military Commander demanded we contract to purchase bottled water for a facility on base, I respectfully declined. In this particular case, the Department of Defense regulations clearly prohibited the purchase of bottled water for stateside bases with only a few exceptions and we did not fit any of the loopholes. (I would have gladly taken a loophole if one was available.)

This order to purchase water was repeated over a period of weeks so I continued to respectfully say "No sir, here is why not and here are some alternatives." The Commander in this story saw my disagreement with his position as disrespect and threatened to discipline me. Others researched the topic as well in an attempt to pull me out of the fire but to no avail. This tense period was only resolved with the Commander's retirement. Although difficult at times, it is entirely possible to disagree and show the right amount of respect at the same time.

Some positional leaders see disagreement much like the emperor in the preceding Hans Christian Andersen story. If someone disagrees with an idea, it is personal and completely out of line. This can lead to what is known as a boss preferring "yes-people." If we all agree too easily, too often, we either have the wrong people on the team, are in serious need of cultural reform or both. Perhaps the culture is hostile to an open exchange of ideas that challenge status quo methods. If we have the wrong people in the mix, they will not contribute openly regardless of the group size. If we have both problems, there is much work to do. It is the responsibility of leaders at all levels to humbly explore input and intent of others. The organizational results will be much better for it.

One step in becoming a military member is to swear or affirm allegiance to the Constitution of the United States. Our constitution defines our most basic ideals and serves as a constant reminder of what our country is about. The military purpose and values link directly to the constitution. In a non-military setting, each for-profit or not-for-profit business has a core purpose and it is essential to remained focused on this. Realize there may be dual purposes where one is stated on a wall plaque and another being the real purpose of what we actually do and how (you should be thinking "culture, culture, culture" by now.) There are many examples over the years of companies that lost their way from their beginnings and either ceased to exist or were swallowed by another entity.

As members of the business community, we must be loyal to the ultimate purpose of our respective organizations. The main reasons for the loyalty are self-preservation and making a long-term difference. Keep in mind there are often disconnects between what is stated and what really occurs. Nevertheless, the smart student of culture will work to understand and act based on environmental awareness. This will cause conflict at times but this disagreement need not be divisive. The charter of an effective culture changer is to be both honest and do so with respect ... all the time. It may not always be easy but it is necessary.

Counsel and Encouragement

Chapter 3 discussed the need for an intentional approach to the use of counsel and encouragement. Seeking true counsel is about wanting honest input from others while asking for encouragement is a request for support or reassurance. It is possible to become at least sloppy or, even worse, ignorant of the differences and roles of each concept. Two opposing but key ideas in *Expected End* are counsel and encouragement. Here are five practical steps to take in applying the use of counsel and encouragement.

(1) Know the difference between counsel and encouragement. Counsel is the meeting of diverse paradigms which in turn urges the participants to explore underlying explanations. Encouragement is the alignment of two or more mental maps or the suspension of a mindset in order to give support. This may reinforce a learning point but will not foster as much growth as counsel. Here are some questions to help. Am I looking more for an ally instead of improvement to a product, process or plan? Will I be overly shocked at a counter point or appreciate the perspective? Am I willing to allow someone else's finger prints on my initiative?

If you want a yes-person's input, just ask for support, encouragement, or reassurance – not input. Be very clear about this point as you will actually gain trust by being honest in your request. If you ask for input, be truly open and reward any disagreeing words if you want such assistance in the future. This requires not only a measured verbal response but a disciplined non-verbal reaction as well (wipe that scowl away, for example).

(2) Seek counsel in order to grow as a leadership student. Engaging in genuine, open dialogue is a guaranteed way to uncover, examine, and improve paradigms. This in turn will ensure a broadened perspective and continuous improvement as a learning leader. It is hard to suspend assumptions to hear another point of view but the effort pays great dividends. The aspiring cultural expert's goal should be to approximate reality as much as possible on any issue and this requires looking for dissimilar perspectives. Not all counsel will be useful but at least take it in and evaluate compared with principles. Here are two examples.

Example 1 – I once asked for and received input on a plan to streamline office processes. Several of us discussed this idea and it went a different direction than I had expected but it was better than my original idea. Upon presenting this plan to the wider audience in the office, one individual said, "You will fail." This set me back momentarily so I re-evaluated the process and plan. In fact, we had arrived at the solution properly and the negative, so-called counsel was based on a person's hidden agenda and not the good of the organization. Thankfully, the initiative worked out fine.

Example 2 – I worked with one team member who I could count on to call me on any dumb ideas. His style was to approach me one-on-one in my office and diplomatically but directly explain the short-sightedness of my plan. The first few times, I found the practice annoying but I quickly grew to value the input as we improved team solutions based on these honest conversations. It also made his encouragement more important as I knew he was completely genuine in his support. I often think of this man's example when needing to give honest feedback I know will cause controversy.

(3) Let encouragement arrive without request (as much as possible). Receiving encouragement or recognition is a human need. In fact, it is appropriate at times to ask for reassurance from a spouse or confidante. It is ideal to keep the requests for encouragement at a moderate level. If I need too much encouragement, there is probably an unmet need for approval indicating a self-esteem problem. It may also indicate a love for status quo and this is poisonous to cultural improvement. If I am producing leadership results in a principled environment, I will not lack for encouragement.

(4) Give counsel based on conscience. This means carefully consider timing, issue significance, and openness of the hearer. This does not mean be timid about giving counsel but rather intentional. This is about being real and generating trust. The best counsel is given at least implicitly in context of the larger organization, whether it is a family, team, company or other organization. Counsel is about making the environment better. Counsel is focused on fostering positive, long-term results and is not beating someone

over the head for sport. Counsel based on conscience is taking an internal moment to listen and determine what is right before giving the input.

(5) Give encouragement only when it is possible to do so genuinely. Given appropriately, specific encouragement will foster intrinsic motivation in others. Conversely, most people can smell flattery or fake praise and this approach will make future words less and less meaningful. Encouragement and counsel both have a role to play in the leader's toolbox. Just be certain to clearly understand each concept and know when and where to properly use the tools.

Continuous Improvement

Innovation and creativity are the fuel of true leaders. This, of course, is a natural progression from examining mindsets and developing good theories. The process can be most invigorating because ideas pop up from unsuspecting places and can be better than expected. The marketplace is changing rapidly and demands a flexible and always-improving response.

An executive who can respond to this exacting and holistic culture change standard will never lack for a place to make a difference. This is much more than just trying harder. This is about different thinking, different action and better results all based on the core values of the organization. (Hopefully, these values are aligned with timeless principles for the ultimate long-term thinking.) Most people want to leave something better than how they found it. To pass on this sort of legacy requires improving the system, not just putting out fires.

An aircraft maintenance commander walked into my office, abruptly sat down and said, "Where is my $300,000? It was on the books yesterday and it is gone today. I want it back." I scrambled for my fire fighter hat.

Over the last several months, I had been fostering an open environment and it was causing some pain at the moment. We were working to shake the smoke-and-mirrors image which meant more conflict at times. In this case, I had no idea what had happened to the $300,000 but began looking. As it turned out, one of the technicians had put the money into another maintenance account so we had not taken it, only moved it without input from the maintenance resource managers. We were still in trouble but not as bad.

Despite occasional heartburn from disgruntled members, I had no regrets opening up the books because we were learning much about our internal processes. We had become so accustomed to how we did business in the past so this was an important way to regain visibility on how customers perceived us.

We recognized our need for updating long-ago buried paradigms and one theory was to use openness as the tool. It worked and we were not deterred by the temporary increase in complaints from newly informed customers.

Too Much Compliance Can Stifle Creativity

No doubt you have noticed how children use imagination at play. Regardless of the props, kids have a way of being unhindered. I remember taking a few hours to build a swing set for our boys and then watch them have more fun with the big, long box.

As we grow older, creativity can tend to become less important as we try to "fit in" at school, work, church, and so on. This is not all bad as a certain amount of conformity is necessary for teamwork and a demonstration of commitment. In fact, in the most disciplined teams, there is clearly a place for compliance. This was certainly the case in flying fighters. The negative part comes when desire for compliance overshadows all else and stifles creative thought. In following orders, be certain to honor the intent over the method. Ultimately, an employee's allegiance must be to the purpose of the organization.

> **In following orders, be certain to honor the intent over the method.**

The innovative thinker is deeply compelled to alignment with what is right (see *Chapter 10*). The ingenious thought comes from a desire to move the organization forward and not simply perpetuate a current method that will eventually disappear in relevance anyway. Here is a negative example.

I once worked for a boss who prized results to the exclusion of most everything else. He was not troubled if we had to treat our people poorly as long as we produced. It was all considered normal in a day's labor. The mentality was "Do not be troubled if I chew you out because you are here to just produce results, and, after all, we are all professionals." The iron expectation of compliance was palatable and the fear component was unmistakable. Culture concerns were mostly irrelevant to this boss and his harsh behavior easily killed creative thought let alone innovative answers.

Innovation, creativity and improvement are all wrapped up with the digging for input from others. Part of the intent is to continually look for new mindsets and begin the process anew. Another purpose is to cause ideas to build on each other and lead to better ways of assisting the culture and then the marketplace. Finally, the dialogue serves to ensure the existing paradigms and theories are complete enough to stand up to the test of real-world application.

Key Points – Chapter 7

1. The better a culture becomes at disciplined conflict, the better the cultural health.
2. Disagreement and disrespect are two, distinct concepts.
3. Counsel produces a collision of paradigms while encouragement reinforces a paradigm. Both counsel and encouragement are necessary in a healthy culture.
4. Continuous improvement demands innovation.
5. Too much compliance can stifle creativity.

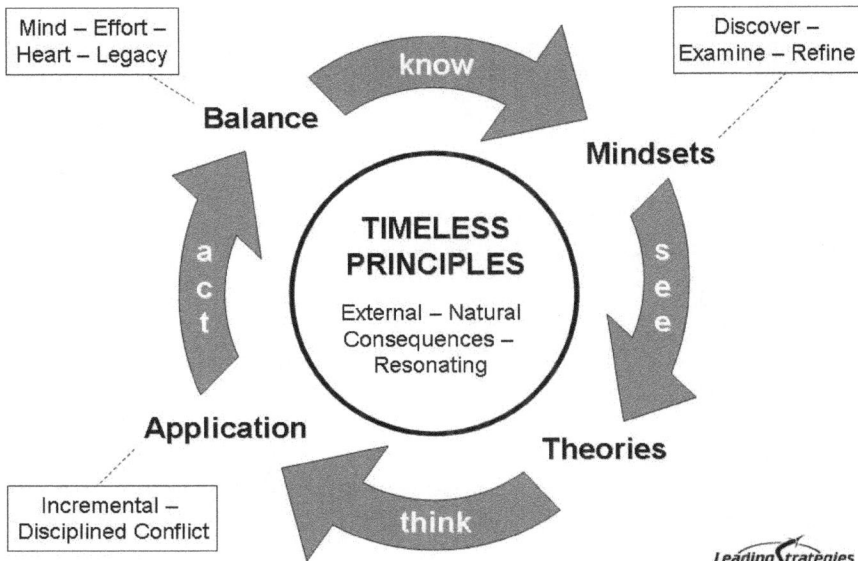

Mind – Effort – Heart – Legacy

know

Balance

Discover – Examine – Refine

Mindsets

TIMELESS PRINCIPLES

External – Natural Consequences – Resonating

a c t

s e e

Application

Incremental – Disciplined Conflict

think

Theories

Leading Strategies

Expected End

Balance

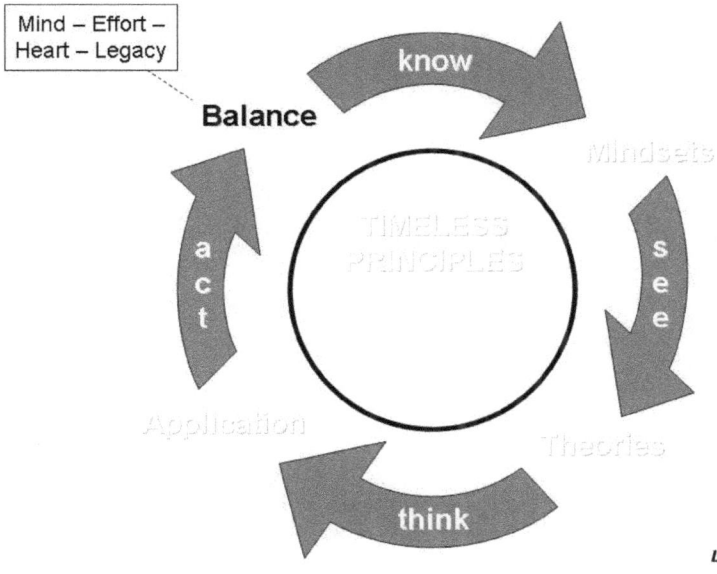

Mind – Effort –
Heart – Legacy

Balance

know

Mindsets

see

TIMELESS
PRINCIPLES

a
c
t

Application

Theories

think

Leading Strategies

Chapter 8

Mind and Effort

In the *Expected End* model, the four elements of balance are mind, effort, heart, and legacy. Balance in this context is needed for an organization to sustain output. Without balance, serious cultural problems will develop over the long-term and hurt results. All four parts of balance are needed and are interconnected with each other. Too much attention on the mind component will create an environment overly logical and detached. Out-of-balance focus on the effort portion produces a busy and perhaps physically exhausting setting where the legacy and heart issues are neglected as well. Look only at the heart section of balance and the environment will probably be too sappy with not enough emphasis on results. Finally, too much interest in the legacy section will cause a business to actually miss leaving a legacy because it neglects present essentials.

Mind – Effectiveness

Just as imagination plays an important role in children's games, highly effective adults use this tool as well. The mind is a busy place or at least it should be. To put it to use in balance is to apply ingenuity to tasks. Anyone can run on auto-pilot and just get through the day. The balanced view goes beyond simply being a passenger in life and asks whether or not this is the best use of time. After refining mindsets, developing theories and then applying, the role of the mind for balance constantly looks at the effectiveness of effort related to the larger environment.

> **The balanced approach always seeks to leverage alternatives into a better solution than simply adding up the parts.**

Effectiveness is an interesting concept and can be taken multiple ways. In our context, effectiveness is a broad measurement always looking at the people involved whether directly or indirectly. How am I impacting others? Am I making a positive difference in the short- and long-term? Am I making things better? Am I building trust?

If focused on climbing the corporate ladder, it can be tempting to evolve into a workaholic. This is to deny the use of an active mind that evaluates the entire environment and compares with the overall long-term goals. Is it more important to make CEO or ensure my kids excel in school? Remember to be cautious of questions that force a choice between one option over another. The balanced approach always seeks to leverage alternatives into a better solution than simply adding up the parts. This requires an active and creative mind.

In addition to creativity, the balanced mind looks for ways to recharge. What are those things that do this? It is important to have a hobby, activity, outlet, other interest or environment to help in this regard. The majority of people periodically need a break from work no matter how much they enjoy the job. Even if you do not need a break, I can all but guarantee you your people need a break from you from time to time. Take appropriate time to enjoy all areas of life and find a higher level of productivity in the workday.

Mind – Reality and Vision

It is natural human behavior to put the best light on things. A cultural student's role is to see the environment as it could be *and* as it is. Said another way, a student of culture is balancing two outwardly conflicting ideas of current reality and future vision. Both roles are vital for effective movement toward the better future. An effective leader will balance seeing things as he or she would wish them to be (vision) while continually diagnosing current reality to have a true starting point. Without this critical skill of seeing current reality and a desired end-state, a culture will not honestly look at mindsets and everything else breaks down from there.

> **A cultural student's role is to see the environment as it could be *and* as it is.**

It is important at this point to emphasize that seeing both current reality and future vision is not negative. Many bosses may view the current reality portion as negativism when the leadership thinker is actually showing loyalty to the organization in an attempt to improve results. These same supervisors may even shun the person they perceive as negative. Seeing current reality is an essential ability for the culture changer and is not negative; it just is.

Several years ago, I was flying an Air Force T-38 Talon very low on fuel. The reason for the low fuel state was another problem: the landing gear (wheels) would not safely extend. I made repeated attempts to properly lower the gear as normally indicated by three lights inside the airplane. This time only two lights illuminated. The ground observer confirmed the gear was extended but he could not be sure they were locked.

Suddenly, I remembered a past emergency simulator session where a landing gear light bulb was bad. I immediately applied this lesson and switched the offending bulb out with another. I now had good indications of a safe landing gear configuration (down and locked).

In this case, my desired vision was to safely land the aircraft but that was greatly threatened by the current reality of an unsafe landing gear indication. Had this emergency continued much longer, I would have been forced to eject from the aircraft as landing with partially extended gear would have been suicide. I had a vision but was forced to deal with current reality to get to the vision. No amount of positive thinking and hopefulness would have made a difference. Action was required.

There is similar human behavior in organizations. A person occupying a leadership position without exercising real leadership likely has hopes and dreams for the business or social agency but refuses to recognize reality. By denying what is, a so-called leader has shut down any chances of organizational improvement in his or her area of influence. The reason is, to quote a mentor, "Bad news does not get better with time." There are very few things that simply improve with the ticking of a clock. Great marriages must be nurtured, fine musicians must practice, and outstanding recipes must be prepared just right. We could make a long list of real-world instances that defy the it-will-get-better-with-time argument. An unbalanced focus on only the future will cause us to not be real in the present. Strangely though, many organizations embrace this dysfunctional paradigm hoping for a magical solution.

> **Ignoring reality has just as significant consequences as dealing with reality.**

Any organization, large or small, profit or not-for-profit, secular or religious, is not exempt from the vision and current reality dynamic. If I sow the seeds of inaction, I will reap an unwelcome crop. If I intentionally sow seeds to move toward the envisioned future, I will be able to start measuring progress. This requires dealing with "what is" right now and working toward alignment with the vision.

Yes, there can be pain in spelling out current reality. Most normal people would rather be comfortable than uncomfortable. Current reality organizational problems usually fall into two categories: (1) They become invisible, or (2) They become sacred cows. Hard to deal with the former and do not touch the latter! Still, reality is not the enemy, it just is. Ignoring reality has just as significant consequences as dealing with reality. The challenge for the effective culture changer is to properly diagnose reality while keeping hope alive in progressing toward a brighter future.

Mind – Systemic Thinking

In thinking about thinking and the mind portion of balance, a growing culture influencer must consider the larger context. It takes the heart component of balance to step back and look. One of my difficult lessons upon being put in charge of a finance area in the military was wearing the bigger hat when out and about at various meetings. Having worked as Budget Director for several years prior, I easily thought about budget considerations but did not do as well with payroll or accounting issues. It is rather obvious that money touches everything in an organization and the military is no different. Invariably, upon returning to the office and sharing what I thought were nice-to-know items, someone in the office would explain the significance of the news. It did not take long until I realized that the question was not "if" a new idea impacted finance but "how." Eventually, I adopted the mindset that everything impacted finance unless proven otherwise. This greatly changed my openness to the environment and in turn improved the finance staff awareness on unit issues.

As any cultural student implements mindsets and theories through application, it is critical to consider the larger impact on the work area and the organization in its broader context by engaging the mind in a systemic process. It is foolhardy to develop a working theory in a vacuum and "just make it happen" only to discover a host of unintended consequences that hurt trust and damage cultural improvement initiatives. A simple question to help in this review is to ask, "How will this new plan impact neighboring employees, areas and departments?" It can sometimes be surprising as to where the natural outcomes will surface. Just remember, depending on the size of the initiative, there are likely more interconnections than obvious at first glance.

Effort

It is amazing what can be done through sheer grit alone. I remember an economics professor in college saying that genius was made up of 10% inspiration and 90% perspiration. In UPT, those of us who were not as talented as others made up the difference with effort. In fact, it was intimidating at times when other noticeably more talented and brighter pilots seemed to glide along with less work or, worse yet, wash out.

Diligent work effort is an important first step but only a first step. The balanced perspective on effort moves to the next phases of doing the right things at the right times. What is most effective? What is the best use of time given my personal and the larger mission? What are the key ways to maintain a personal or organizational system that works well and is not just a brute force machine.

> **Effort in the balanced sense is carving spaces out of the schedule for personal and organizational recharging.**

The balanced mindset of effort then asks the question of how to renew the system that produces the effort? How can we increase the effort capacity? This analysis requires stepping back from the fray, stopping just going through the motions and determining a better way of working.

Effort in the balanced sense is carving spaces out of the schedule for personal and organizational recharging. It is all too easy in our fast-paced era to push the output at the exclusion of most other priorities. Balance demands a healthier approach that keeps a solid look to the long-term and to the other elements of balance (mind, heart and legacy).

Effort – Work Environment Awareness

As with other areas of the *Expected End* model, awareness is a necessary part of balance in order to measure progress. Work environment awareness is so dynamic and yet the committed student of culture must be in tune as much as possible. Searching for and clarifying organizational mindsets naturally leads to greater environmental awareness by the leader. What is morale like? What is it like on different topics? Who is an unreasonable supervisor? What departments have lower than average turnover? Who are the quietly, rising stars?

It is amazing what a supervisor can learn by fostering a pattern of regularly chatting with all members on the team. There is data all over just waiting to be discovered even in the seeming innocent conversation about a football game last weekend or grandma's quilting club activities. A growing student of organizational climate must be attuned to all the information that is broadcast. Treat it like the solid gold it is. In addition to building trust through genuine interest, the conversation will often naturally move to work topic concerns. What obstacles are highly frustrating to this individual? What themes will develop upon talking with several people in the same area? Why do the issues matter? What company mindsets drive the behavior? Balance is greatly boosted through continual environmental scanning. What are all the clues saying? What is the message that yearns to be heard?

Effort – Keep Flying

When a pilot encounters any type of emergency situation, the natural tendency is to focus too much attention on the emergency. There is more than one story of an aviator too distracted with a problem to fly safely. As a beginning Air Force pilot, I will never forget a simulator flight where I became so distracted from basic flying, I ran into a mountain. The instructor's admonition of, "You would be dead right now if you had been in an airplane" was very sobering.

In the business setting, most of us do not have the privilege of shutting down the machine to redesign and rebuild it to meet the latest marketplace needs. The company must continue operating as we do our respective leadership work. This means continuing to influence what should be accomplished today while honoring timeless principles (see *Chapter 10*) and nonstop improvement. This also translates to constantly evaluating if the current movement aligns with mission objectives. This is not about feel-good but about results. This is about meeting competitive demands in our very fast-paced economy, regardless of the organization type. It takes courage but it is a critical skill for the cultural student to consistently do the right things.

Effort – Be Decisive

Staying true to the effort portion of balance calls for good decision making. To illustrate, finding a solution to an aircraft emergency requires making constant and timely decisions. A pilot can only make decisions based on what is seen, heard and felt (e.g., airframe vibrations, extra weight on the flight controls, etc.). In many cases, a wingman can take a look at a crippled airplane to give any additional data. Otherwise, it is time to analyze the problem and move toward a solution. Several years ago, when an engine fire indicator came on in the F-4 I was flying, I immediately turned toward the home airport. This sounds basic and yet many a student pilot has wasted precious minutes in a simulator by working through the checklist before turning the airplane toward a suitable landing patch.

Decision-making is a skill any successful business person will possess and build. A wise leadership instructor once said, "Intent counts more than technique." His point was to make timely decisions for the good of the organization even if your technique is not perfect. The only people who have 100% of the data for a decision are historians (and that might even be debatable). Do not overly labor on a decision: Make it. It is guaranteed to teach something in the process to the open student. This is particularly true if the choice turns out to be a blunder. If there are too few decisions, there is also very little learning going on. Stay aligned with mission, vision, and values but, by all means, make a decision.

Decisiveness helps balance by decreasing the time required to execute. While it is unwise to be rash at decision points, it adds quality to the setting to make reasonable decisions with reasonable speed. There is somewhat of an art form to this but each culture student will discover a good balance in time if he or she is open to feedback.

Effort – Be Flexible

Finding balance in a cultural sense is the ultimate multi-task action; decisive yet flexible; in the moment yet thinking long-term and about legacy. Balanced effort is much more than working harder; it is clearly working smarter.

Now flexibility might seem to contradict the previous point but speaks to how things can change without much warning. What if my plan does not work? One rainy winter day, I landed an F-4 with the hook down because of a hydraulic failure. (The Navy guys out there are laughing.) The firm touchdown went as planned but the hook bounced over the approach-end cable. Fortunately, my Weapons System Officer (WSO or backseater) and I had discussed this possibility prior to the landing and had already decided to stay on the runway to catch the opposite end cable due to several other factors. Had we missed again, we would have ejected from the aircraft. We caught the opposite end cable. Whew.

One tongue-in-cheek saying in the Air Force is "flexibility is the key to airpower." Regardless of how pretty the strategic plan looks, there will be points to improvise along the way. This is where knowing and living principled values pays big dividends. Stick to decisions as much as practical but do not run the company train over a cliff for sake of personal ego or a written treatise. If the market needs change, adapt. Make another decision. Be flexible.

Flexibility enhances balance because it allows for meeting changing demands as they occur. Resist wishy-washy but be attuned to all that is happening in application and flex as needed to stay on track for the desired outcomes. One way to help avoid vacillating too much is to constantly examine the underlying mindsets and theories. Upon finding flaws under the current activity, modify the approach a bit to stay focused on results. This is not to suggest pursuing goals half-hearted; just be smart and ready to improve a good plan with great execution.

Effort – Have An Out

Continuing in the flexibility vein, having an out is necessary to maintain balanced effort. An analogy here is related to formation flying of two or more aircraft. One of the staples of formation flying is the rejoin where one airplane overtakes another aircraft with speed, geometry or both. Every good formation flier always has an out in case an unexpected collision becomes imminent. Having an out is more than just in the moment but is thoughtful and planned well ahead of the problem. In the military aviation setting, we actually sat and talked at different times about various scenarios and the possible responses. This type of discussion can happen months and years before the actual problem occurs.

In military formation flying, there is always a designated formation leader but the reality is that all pilots in the formation have basic responsibilities to keep all flight members safe. A nice rejoin concluding with a mid-air collision will ruin anybody's day, hence, the "what if" and "have an out." No matter how the rejoin may be going, a savvy aviator will be constantly assessing and adjusting not only the rejoin maneuver but the Plan B should something go very wrong. Fighting other airplanes requires more aggressive use of geometry although the same basic rules of a rejoin apply.

I remember a time as a new F-4 driver when in the thick of a practice fight, there were two of us unknowingly converging on the same target, belly to belly. I thought I was going to be a hero. Thankfully I had an experienced backseater who yelled, "Belly check!" Upon rolling inverted and seeing the imminent mid-air, I wracked the airplane in an opposite direction and we all lived to fight another day.

As the positional leader or culture student, you may or may not want to admit a Plan B publicly to risk distracting or demoralizing your team members. You may not always have an elegant or fully developed alternative. Be always thinking ahead as it may be an out by phases or incrementally. Again, just like in flying, having an out is more than a reaction in the moment but is the leader being several steps ahead of the non-leaders. (Remember this is about thinking, not positions.) Having an out is really an extension on the flexibility theme but our era demands this approach. If all our grand schemes fall apart, what will we do? How will we recover to keep the enterprise viable? How will we rally the "troops" to pick up the pieces? Nimbleness is a critical core competency and an effective leader will demonstrate it by staying several steps ahead of those being lead.

The Balance Connection – Mind and Effort

Here is how mind and effort are connected to application. Please recall that balance directs us to consider mind, effort, heart and legacy. Here is a summary of the first two parts.

Mind – Balance is enhanced by an engaged mind that uses imagination, creativity, and mission evaluation. The balanced mind view is constantly deciding, assessing and, most importantly, deeply thinking about paradigms and theories. How can we do this more efficiently and cost-effective? The mind cares deeply about the product and service. We would have sloppy outputs without engaged minds. Also, it is necessary to keep mind perspectives fresh by cultivating hopeful curiosity.

Effort – Actions contribute to balance by relieving the tension of pent-up ideas. Balanced effort is more than spreading available resources over all responsibilities. Effort that is balanced constantly makes choices and priorities. This can be compared to painting a room. Paint to cover based on the amount of paint, not the size of the room. Buy more paint if necessary but do not attempt to make a pint work where a gallon is needed.

Further, balanced effort is divided into meeting short-term deadlines, medium-terms goals while also working toward long-term vision. Effort is parceled out very carefully to ensure the entire time spectrum is serviced. Paradoxically, effort is conducted with vigor to support the desired ends. To help in considering the time factor, consider the timeline below. In general, the timeframe for a leader is longer than a person who does not think in a leadership perspective. For the leadership and cultural student, we will assume the short-term is defined by any timeframe up to a few months. Four months up to three to five years define medium term and long-term is made up of timelines of greater than the three to five year span. Finally, and most importantly, effort is about renewal and recharging the system so it can continue to produce the desired service or products long-term.

Leadership Timeline

Up to a few months	4 months up to 3-5 years	Beyond 3-5 years
Short Term	**Medium Term**	**Long Term**

> ## Key Points – Chapter 8
> 1. Two of the four parts of balance are the areas of mind and effort.
> 2. Balance in the mind aspect is creative planning.
> 3. Balance in an effort approach is intentional activity to include renewal and servicing the complete timeline.

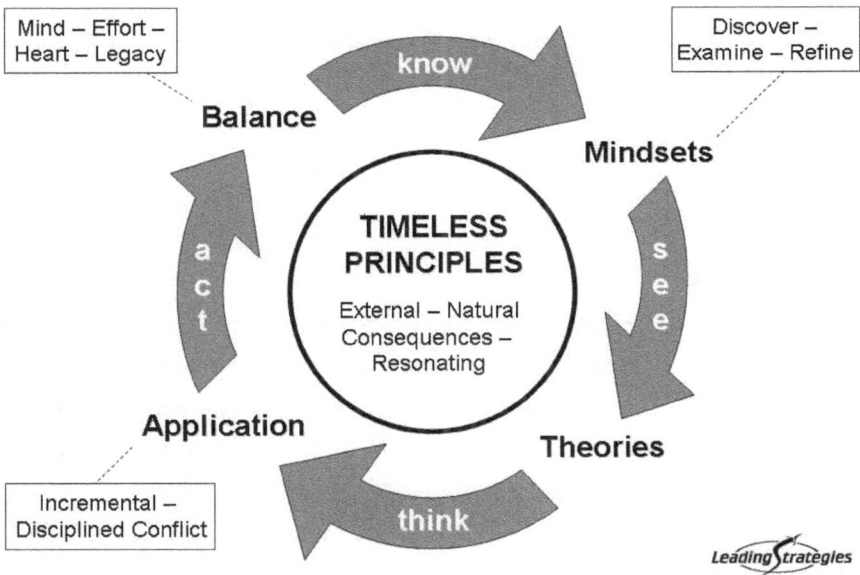

Mind – Effort – Heart – Legacy

Balance

know

Discover – Examine – Refine

Mindsets

act

TIMELESS PRINCIPLES

External – Natural Consequences – Resonating

see

Application

Incremental – Disciplined Conflict

think

Theories

Leading Strategies

Chapter 9

Heart and Legacy

The lessons of *Expected End* often appear opposed to each other on the surface. Ideas like long-term and short-term, honesty and respect, counsel and encouragement are just a few examples. The balance approach of the heart looks deeper than the surface to find the common areas between two or more seemingly opposed initiatives.

Heart – Consideration and Toughness

The introduction to having balance in a heart sense is to consistently use consideration combined with toughness. The trait of consideration is often ignored in business relations because we typically stand in awe at the tough business man or woman who has a take-no-prisoners persona. Possibly this is a carryover from our respect for the rugged individualism of U.S. history. Regardless, toughness must be balanced with consideration for a healthy

110

culture that will give back. So much comes down to balance. A positional leader who is considerate but not tough will give the store away. A company negotiator who is tough without any consideration can easily slip over into unethical territory.

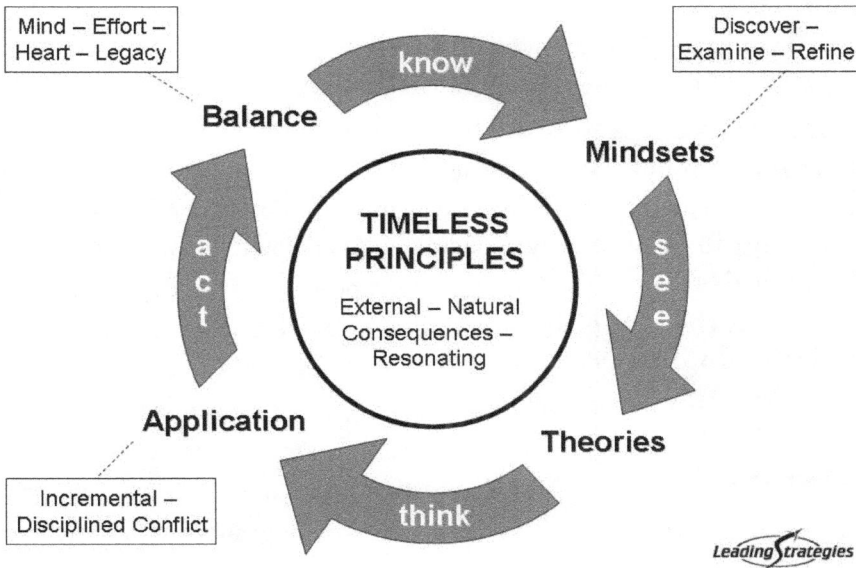

The Colonel I mention at the beginning of the Introduction personified a balance between toughness and consideration. He proved excellent at holding himself and others accountable while cultivating very positive relations with all around. When I attended his retirement ceremony years later (he was a General by then), there were several stories that showed his consistent ability to balance seemingly opposed concepts such as being tough while showing consideration to others. I have additional positive stories in my own memory as do many other people.

Heart – Process

Another part of the balanced approach with heart is process. The heart is more focused on the process and overall effectiveness instead of efficiency. The empathic method looks at the smaller task in context of the larger objective. The heart cares about results but it cares more about process. The heart is better at interrupting a script to meet the more inclusive systemic desire. In short, the heart sees the forest and trees.

Balance in this context means slowing the frantic pace just a bit in order to sustain production. Several years ago, I turned on the news while driving in the car and was shocked to hear a newsflash of an F-4 accident in my squadron. I immediately drove to the base to offer what help possible. That day, one of our fellow aviators was killed with another severely injured. It was a very sobering time and a reminder that despite all the adrenaline in flying fighters, we were still mere mortals.

> **Having heart is about caring for the organization and the individual at the same time.**

In the first few hours, there was only speculation on what really had happened to bring an airplane and crew down. Not surprisingly, the normal macho and bantering environment was much subdued. We did have hearts and several of us were doing some soul-searching about the potential cost of flying high performance aircraft day in and day out. More importantly to the organization, we took a fresh look at the process of flying fighters on macro and micro levels.

Balance in a heart sense looks at how we are doing business. What are all the consequences of our actions, not just the physical product or service? How do we impact the families of our workers? How do we affect other companies? What positive contributions are we making to the lives of people in general? How are we doing in a broader sense than just work?

Heart – Long-Term

Because "heart" in the balanced sense focuses more on process and product, a long-term outlook is a natural consideration. Long-term has a way of giving perspective that other tools may not because it holds us more accountable. It is possible to get away with a lot in the short-term. For instance, I can treat others roughly, cheat on my expense reports and not maintain my equipment or tools. Chances are that none of these actions will cause much damage in the near-term. However, it is obvious these actions will cause harm given enough time. This is why heart matters and why long-term is so important.

If an airplane is in trouble, it is normal for the pilot to want to land as soon as practical. Despite the urgency, there are questions to consider that will make or break the outcome. What is the fuel state? What is the nearest field that can appropriately handle the aircraft emergency? How far to the ideal airport? What is the weather like at the intended landing airport?

So often, it is easy to be too caught up with the urgent priorities of the present while all but forgetting the long-term. Executing a flawed business plan perfectly will still assure the eventual failure of the business. We must consider questions like to where will our current organizational behavior lead? What changes are needed to arrive at the preferred destination? What business are we really in ... long-term? How should the firm change to meet fickle consumer demands? How should we

> **It is the job of a culture changer to devote sufficient time to future work.**

shape internal succession plans? How are we educating and growing the up-and-coming leaders to meet their future challenges? Of course, there are many more questions as well.

The long-term may seem far away but it is as or more important than the present for the culture leader. Chances are you can count a large number of people who do their best work in the present. Do not forget future years. It is the job of a culture changer to devote sufficient time to future work.

The cultural student absolutely must devote some brain time to the long-term. There are any number of societal pressures to make a decision for the immediate need alone. The thought continues that we will worry about the long-term when we get there. Sadly, the long-term destination is influenced long before we arrive there by all the earlier, smaller decisions.

The would-be culture watcher who gets caught up in short-term myopia will not be as successful as one who looks out into the future and bases decisions on the long-term good. This process runs a decision "down the tracks" to try and predict how the decision will play out farther than the immediate horizon. Considering the long-term in decision making is similar to comparing current reality and future vision but is broader. Implementing this concept may feel unnatural at first but it is a mandatory skill for the cultural student. Notice how the time frames below are flexible.

Leadership Timeline

Up to a few months	4 months up to 3-5 years	Beyond 3-5 years
Short Term	**Medium Term**	**Long Term**

Legacy – Any length beyond your tenure

For example, flying an aircraft "cross-country" meant traveling from one city to another much like taking an airline flight. While flying an F-4 across a couple states to Davis-Monthan Air Force Base, Arizona, my Weapons System Officer (WSO) and I encountered heavier than expected upper level winds blowing against us. This meant we were traveling slower over the ground than anticipated and were using more fuel than planned.

As we continually updated calculations, the planned fuel amount at our destination continued to shrink. So we had a choice to make: should we land short of destination to take on more fuel or could we make up some of the shortage by flying at a more efficient speed and altitude (height above the ground)? We determined that we could reasonably make the destination by adjusting how we were flying (a little slower for example to use less fuel).

Notice we were making decisions based on the long-term or end-goal. Had we decided to ignore the destination scenario and just fly for the fun of it, we would have made an emergency landing short of our intended airfield. Making decisions with only the immediate or near-term in mind only increases the inevitable long-term cost. In many cases, this cost will occur after the short-sighted manager moves on.

Legacy

In the past, legacy usually meant beyond long-term. However, in our mobile society, the time-frame related to legacy varies greatly. Regardless of time in a role, most people want to leave the people and things they care for better than they found them. It is all about making a positive difference and is a natural human desire. The argument of balance demands we take a close look at long-term actions linked to legacy even if our time in a particular position is not long-term. Legacy ensures we look beyond ourselves whether this is relatively short- or long-term. One caution: overly focusing on legacy at the exclusion of other parts of balance will result in an approach that "chases its tail" or forgets the others parts of the model as well as timeless principles. Consider legacy and do so in concert with the other parts of balance. How will this decision improve the system after I leave? Can other principled people build on my approach with greater success? Will my style pave the way for future innovation by others? Am I growing a personal kingdom or an organizational culture? Filter decisions through the prism of legacy to find results that will go the distance.

The Balance Connection – Heart and Legacy

The bottom line question should be, "how does balance improve application?" Balance greatly enhances application by filling it out. We could compare application without balance to malnourishment. Without proper nutrition, an unhealthy person or animal can do things and functions to some degree but not anywhere near the true potential. Upon advancing in health, stamina improves, strength increases and mental engagement goes up dramatically. The same can be said for any business, agency, or non-profit organization.

Here is the summary of how balanced heart and legacy are brought to bear upon application. Remember heart and legacy plus mind and effort (in the previous chapter) are necessary to achieve a true balanced approach.

Heart – Balance grows in perspective with heart. The more heart is involved, the more the company is concerned about the process to deliver the product or service. The way we accomplish something is important. Process matters to a healthy culture.

Legacy – The big "why" questions are always part of leaving a legacy. Yes, we must produce something to stay in business whether it is a product or service and yes we must put consideration into the process. But why does it matter? What will happen after we move on or pass on? Balance from a legacy standpoint keeps the work in perspective. Legacy keeps us from just being busy for its own sake.

In some ways, balance is always elusive as we never find perfect balance all the time. Despite this fact, it is entirely possible to find satisfying levels of balance even while improving. Balance buffs up the 90-pound weakling of mediocre effort and moves a culture toward greatness. Balance provides both intrinsic and extrinsic rewards. The savvy cultural changer recognizes the importance. Balance moves the student of culture from acting to knowing and there is a big difference.

Key Points – Chapter 9
1. Two of the four parts of balance are the areas of heart and legacy.
2. A balanced heart approach is big picture consideration.
3. A balanced legacy approach is the long-term aligned with mission, vision and values portion.

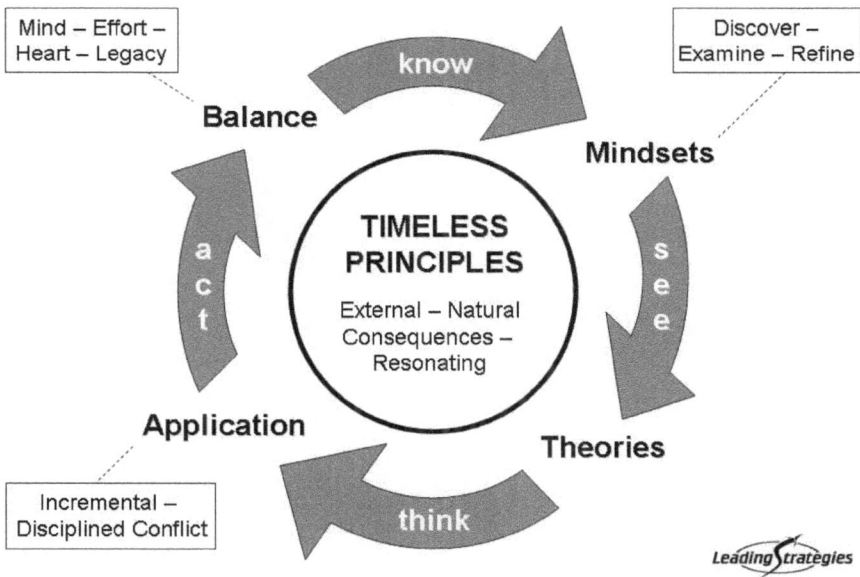

Mind – Effort – Heart – Legacy

Discover – Examine – Refine

know

Balance

Mindsets

a c t

TIMELESS PRINCIPLES

External – Natural Consequences – Resonating

s e e

Application

Theories

Incremental – Disciplined Conflict

think

Leading Strategies

Expected End

Timeless Principles

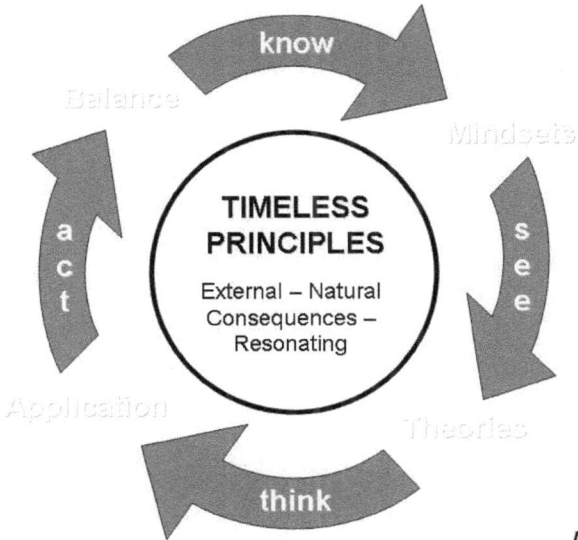

Chapter 10

A Solid Core

Over the years of our lives, we become aware of diversity in value, thought and action. Each culture, whether of a family, organization or country, has its own personality and unique characteristics. There are norms within each culture that regulate behavior and determine what is generally accepted. This is both good and bad and beauty is definitely in the eye of the beholder. The agenda of the *Expected* End model is to find common sense ideas to improve cultural health. The new methods may be perceived by some as uncomfortable or bad but change is an integral part of making and keeping cultures healthy. The point to emphasize here is the importance of using timeless principles in any of these experiments. Without principles in place, the changes will be change for its own sake and will likely fail. This all takes time, persistence and a reliable basis on which to make such transitions. Timeless principles are a non-negotiable part of the *Expected End* model because without principles, the model does not stand.

Speaking of change, I learned first-hand in the 1980s and 1990s that Air Force pilots occupied the top spots in the food chain of the organization. To take it a step farther, fighter pilots viewed themselves as the best of the best and while this attitude can be annoying in social settings, it is necessary in the airplane. As with any organization, the Air Force culture is changing with advancing technology and evolving global threats. One change that has sent shock waves through some quarters in the military flying community is the remote controlled airplane. While it is a natural progression to add this type of unpiloted vehicle to the military arsenal, assigning former fighter pilots to exchange highly maneuverable, powerful fighter airplanes for remote control joysticks, television monitors and office chairs can be ego-busting. Perhaps this helps the reader imagine high-ranking and well-intentioned people arguing over whether remote aircraft should have a significant role in the future of the Air Force. This transition is similar to the heated arguments in the 1900s about whether or not aircraft had a role at all in the future of military warfare.

Any personal or organizational response to changing times will be dictated by a foundation of values. If I am defined by my position, a job change will shatter my world. If I bring a sense of enduring purposes to any position, change is less painful.

A Case for a Foundation

My wife and I built a house recently and learned a number of lessons throughout. The most grueling phase was the foundation. On the day the excavator dug out the building site, it began to rain very hard and set a record for precipitation over the next few days. Of course, since this was the beginning of the wet season, the soggy factor did not improve for several months.

As we moved ahead with ground work, there were times when my commitment was weak. Cold, wet and muddy, I would try to convince myself that surely it was good enough now. But I was learning an old lesson in a new setting that "just OK" is not enough for a literal foundation let alone in a figurative sense.

As unglamorous as it may be, the hidden preparation work and core is essential. The character of your heart will come out over time and particularly in the difficult turns of life. Cheat on the prep work and the project will suffer eventually. It may not be obvious at first but it will happen nonetheless.

Shifting Sand

I served as a pastor for a time where the church building had a lot of shifting due to inadequate ground preparation during initial construction. The building was of beautiful design and served our needs well except for the problems associated with settling. Over the years, an increasing number of windows would not operate because they were stuck in the frames. The maintenance man needed to periodically plane some of the doors so they would still open and close. The impact of insufficient ground work was invisible on the day the church was dedicated but was painfully apparent to those of us meeting in the structure over 20 years later.

Foundation matters and the reality is we all have one. The question then is what materials are in your model? Some will choose the slippery slope of relative ethics that just point to what is expedient in the here and now. Others may decide that values of any type are an old fashioned idea for an earlier era and you can merely make decisions based on what feels good at the moment. While these and a wide variety of other approaches may at least fill the void for some type of temporary foundational work, they will not hold up to the strains of a lifetime full of decisions. As people, we need a code of ethics, set of values, or other standard on which to make decisions. We all have values of one sort or another. What set is most effective and how do we determine this effectiveness? The short answer is

> **Foundation matters and the reality is we all have one. The question then is what materials are in your model?**

timeless principles are the only option that will survive long-term. For our purposes, timeless principles are defined below.

Timeless Principles

- External and non-negotiable – We cannot control, add to or delete principles from this list; we cannot outlaw principles any more than we can outlaw gravity
- Natural consequences – Principles yield predictable and consistent outcomes over the long-term
- Resonating – The various principles strike a chord with most people worldwide as basic standards of right and wrong

---

The more decisions and actions are aligned with principles, the greater level of effectiveness. The opposite is true as well. Examples of principles can be found in the Bible and include excellence, respect, integrity, courage, kindness, loyalty, commitment, honesty, service, humor, forgiveness, teamwork, renewal, patience, faith, persistence, charity, diligence, and consideration. All the other parts of the *Expected End* model depend on this core.

Super Principle #1 – Trust

The root of all effective human relationships is trust. All relationships have trust in some form or another or else the bond will not last. Trust is so pivotal to all human interaction and is a business imperative. Those who scoff at building and maintaining trust in a business or other setting do so at their own peril. Productivity and creativity are higher when trust is valued. If trust is not important, productivity and creativity will become sluggish and eventually disappear. If we are honest with ourselves, most of us have worked in both environments and can attest to the consequences.

Most people know that treating others with trust and respect will bring very positive outcomes and yet how many of us struggle to do just this? Many of us could make an impassioned argument for the importance of great communication (to include deep listening) only to find ourselves moving too quickly past a conversation with a spouse, child or co-worker. What did she say? What did he mean? These and other questions are all important to process carefully in the moment.

> **Productivity and creativity are higher when trust is valued. The opposite is just as true.**

Since we are talking about timeless principles, the natural effects of a trusting or non-trusting scenario happen whether we want them or not. One of the non-negotiable elements of a healthy environment is trust and it is one of two "super-principles." Everything rises or falls on this element. A closely-related second piece we previously addressed is communication because trust is built, maintained or torn down by the exchange of words and ideas.

Trust and Leadership

Why is trust important to leadership and healthy cultures? Without trust, individuals are not open with each other. They hide behind a façade for personal protection. In spite of outward bravado, most people gravitate toward those they can enjoy on some level in a two-way exchange. In any healthy human relationship there is a basic question under the surface that says, "How much do you care about me?" Most people will not maintain a long-term friendship with someone who belittles them, tears them down or devalues them. We have all worked at some point for a boss who was impossible to please. You can be sure there was some sort of negative reaction going on first internally and then sometimes externally.

Think back to that boss who was always unreasonable and treated you poorly. What if he or she would have approached you asking for input on an upcoming project? If you knew your ideas were consistently not valued or used, how likely would you have been to contribute openly? You might have made some helpful comments depending on your personal values but probably stopped short of full input.

On the other hand, think back to working for a boss who brought the best out of you. This person consistently appreciated participation and implemented at least some of your thoughts into a final solution. Now, how likely would you be to offer thoughts on an upcoming task? It was probably hard to shut you up! Why the difference between the two scenarios? In one word: trust. Over time, most healthy people do not gladly go where uninvited in relationships.

> **Collective paradigms bind together for powerful discussions leading to incredible solutions.**

Now try to imagine how trust impacts a team grappling with a problem. With low trust, members are suspicious of other's agendas. Individuals will posture and jockey for what is most self-serving instead of the task at hand. With high trust on the other hand, each person is fully engaged and valued. More importantly, the collective paradigms bind together for powerful discussions leading to incredible solutions. Most of us are attracted to the latter environment of high trust. After all, it is good, clean adult fun to be part of a great solution for the betterment of the team as a whole.

The idea of promoting high trust is not to advocate an over-sensitive atmosphere or one that is too "sappy." Plastic interaction can be more annoying than other dysfunctional behaviors. The theme is for the benefit of the enterprise. Taken in a principled context, this is an inspiring challenge to all who want to leave something better than they found it.

It all starts with a mindset. Based on how I see the circumstances, what is a reasonable way to respond to the needs? How can I incorporate a method into business to make a difference? Trust will do the heavy lifting in creating a great work climate so learn how to excel at building trust to expand influence in changing culture for the better.

Building and Maintaining Trust

It takes considerate and courageous communication in order to build trust: considerate because it shows I value you and what you contribute to the mix; courageous because most people can detect authenticity or the lack thereof. If someone is less than authentic, it makes others wonder 'why' and be suspicious of a hidden agenda. On the other hand, if someone is a what-you-see-is-what-you-get person in a considerate way, trust builds. (I can believe this person and this person is really interested in working with me.)

Another important part of building and maintaining trust is to make and keep commitments. As a team evaluates how to achieve long-range goals, group players will need to participate and this is where commitment comes in. Making a pledge is great but is only half the equation. It is essential for the member to keep the commitment otherwise, it would have been better to not have made the promise in the first place.

Of course, doing the opposite of the building and maintaining trust will lead to sabotaging trust in relationships. This may stem from simple lack of attention versus ill will. This reinforces why the developing student must constantly cultivate self-awareness. High-impact solutions are made from high-trust relationships.

While some may look down on the value of trust, it is a force multiplier that must be cultivated in all organizations desiring to produce outstanding results. There certainly are organizations that operate and make money without high-trust. How much more profitable would they be with improved trust? There are

> **High-impact solutions are made from high-trust relationships.**

companies who insist on loyalty when in reality the expectation is one-way: up. This demoralizes trust and compromises effective results, regardless of the business.

High Quality Relationships

Remember, effective leadership will rise or fall on trusting relationships. Cultural advances in turn are produced by this leadership because connecting with others in a high-trust fashion creates a premium working environment with high-impact solutions. Trust and results are patently tied together and the connection is undeniable. An informal leader who highly values trusting relationships will only increase in effectiveness upon assuming a more formal role.

More specifically, how willing is the team to put out extra effort for a looming deadline if you have built high-trust relationships with them? They know you will easily hand out credit to all involved and you value them for all they bring to the mix. They also know you are not manipulating them or taking unreasonable advantage of their skills. These members will be vested in the outcome.

> **Trust and results are patently tied together.**

Super Principle #2 – Humility

In seeking to learn new things and improve culture, the student comes face-to-face with the realization there is so much more to know out there than is humanly possible. No matter how wise we may think we are or how practiced we may become in any given area, there is still more to know. The vastness of our reality prospects greatly dwarf our ability to absorb.

Interestingly, the student of culture takes inspiration from this enormous vista and enjoys the adventure of exploration while holding to a true sense of humility. The benefit of humility is it allows a student to truly be a student open and hungry for learning. A lack of humility will inhibit the growth of anyone as the paradigm of excessive pride is satisfied with the current circumstance. It is automatic: Stop being humble and stop learning; start being humble and find a huge supply of wisdom. Humility is the second of two super-principles.

As critical as humility-generated learning is to cultural health, humility-generated trust is all the more beneficial in relationships. A humble attitude among others draws them in, especially in boss-to-employee relations. Humility between people personifies two-way respect and creates a bond that lifts a team far above what it would be otherwise.

Principled Living

My family and I lived for a time in a home built in 1915 that did not have a traditional foundation. However, there was a series of stout beams on top of well-prepared ground to undergird the structure. The system worked as this house was in an area of California prone to earthquakes (we experienced a few while living there). The point is the non-traditional approach honored the structural requirements to keep the house solid and the occupants safe.

> **Stop being humble and stop learning; start being humble and find a huge supply of wisdom.**

In honoring timeless principles, positive consequences take care of themselves. Style becomes secondary because principled living is in every action. The more holistic the approach in following principles, the better the outcome. For instance, if I live by the principle of love but neglect accountability, my life and relationships will be out of balance whether in a family or work setting. Children who are loved without any accountability will grow up overly self-centered and will struggle to become productive citizens of society. For best results, live by as many principles simultaneously as possible.

Timeless Principles and Culture

Without timeless principles firmly in place, the cultural model of this book becomes just another technique that will fail more than work. Timeless principles are the core and determine the effectiveness of the other parts of the model. To be clearer, let's connect principles to each of the other four stops in the model.

Mindsets – Timeless principles such as respect, honesty, loyalty and integrity make a significant difference in the process of searching for, finding, exploring and modifying mindsets. Without these principles firmly in place, the mindset explorer will be prone to unethical manipulation, hidden agendas, power plays and the like. It is imperative the cultural

> **For best results, live by as many principles simultaneously as possible.**

explorer be certain of a principled basis before exploring for mindsets or else there will be many unintended and negative consequences in relationships.

Theories – In this category, principles such as honesty, openness and curiosity assure the development of robust theories that work in a variety of situations. The stronger the theory, the better the application or the doing. A haphazard theory developed through self-serving pride and unwillingness to explore approaches in technique will doom the thinker to shoddy results. Openness is intended here to mean a willingness to consider additional evidence on alternative methods or techniques. Openness for this context does not mean a desire to consider any theory that is not plainly principle-based. In other words, the ends do not always justify the means regardless of how admirable the ends may be.

Application – Diligence and excellence are two examples of the many principles that easily link to application. Working diligently and with excellence in all aspects of life will ensure success that will last a lifetime and beyond. An easy example is cultivating a garden. A person who carefully takes care of the garden in every way to include site selection, climate consideration, soil composition, plant spacing, watering, fertilizing and weeding will reap a bountiful harvest. Ignore one or more of these elements and the garden results will suffer. Principles always hold and we only get to indirectly choose the outcomes. The here-and-now choices are whether or not to align with principles as we grow in understanding of them.

Balance – Variety, planning, and renewal are three principles attached to balance. For example, if supporting my family financially is a good thing, how much time should I spend at this endeavor? How much time is too much? Should I camp out at work? At what point would I become irrelevant to my family all in the name of simply providing for their basic physical needs? To continue, if loving my family means spending time with them and attending to their every need, how much time should I expend here? And so the questions go on. Moderation by its very nature seeks continual balance between all parts of an environment realizing there may be temporary imbalances from time to time. Planning is one form of balance renewal. Balance expects we will spend appropriate times doing all daily activities as well as making time to recharge to maintain the highest operating efficiency. Every person is different in how the principle of renewal is applied but every person needs downtime of some sort. Remember, we ignore principled living at our own peril.

Key Points – Chapter 10

1. Base all decisions on timeless principles.
    a. Principles are permanent and external to us.
    b. Living for or against principles has predictable outcomes.
    c. Principles strike a chord within most people (resonate).
2. Trust will make or break a culture.
3. Humility is one of the most important traits for learning and trust-building.
4. Live by as many principles simultaneously as possible.
5. There are two super-principles: trust and humility.

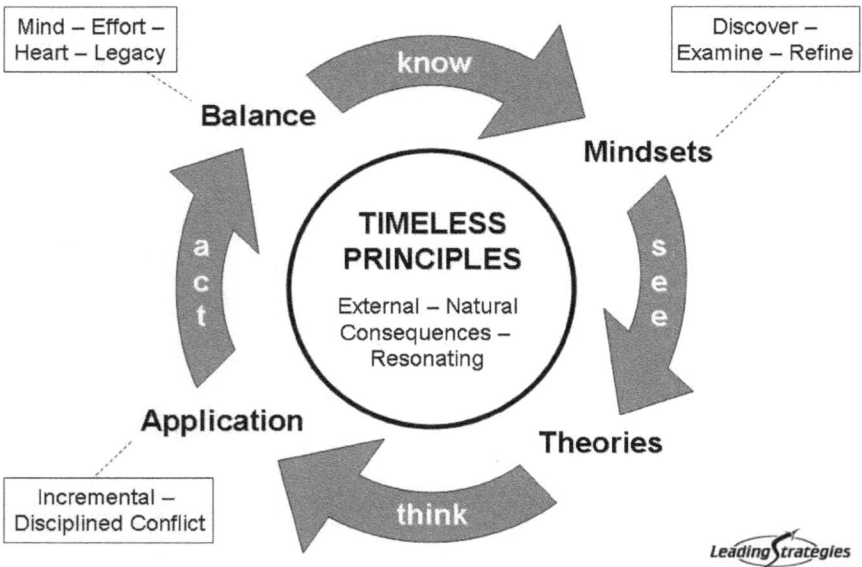

Mind – Effort – Heart – Legacy

Discover – Examine – Refine

Balance

know

Mindsets

TIMELESS PRINCIPLES

External – Natural Consequences – Resonating

act

see

Application

Theories

Incremental – Disciplined Conflict

think

Leading Strategies

Closing Thoughts

Reaching cultural excellence through principled leadership is not a destination but a lifelong pursuit. In the *Expected End* model, the cycle goes on and on with ever-increasing quality of results. In other words, the journey is far from complete after making one, two or three complete revolutions from *mindsets* through *balance* all revolving around timeless principles. The good news is as the student becomes more adept at using the model, movement from one point to the next will often be faster than in the past. Use caution though as building a healthier culture is never about speed alone. Quality is more important than speed and what may seem slow at first will often yield results faster than expected.

Also keep in mind the learner will easily be at different points in the model at the same time on different issues. Maybe you find yourself farther into the model in your family life and still struggling at the mindset level at work. Perhaps you are highly balanced in a volunteer capacity but would like to move into more application with your spouse. Real life is never as easy, clean or simple as in a book. Resist the urge to just "fill the square" and claim the title without having the substance. Leadership is a way of thinking and very intrinsically rewarding. Upon adopting the new paradigm, you may be surprised where you do and do not observe quality leadership in any organization.

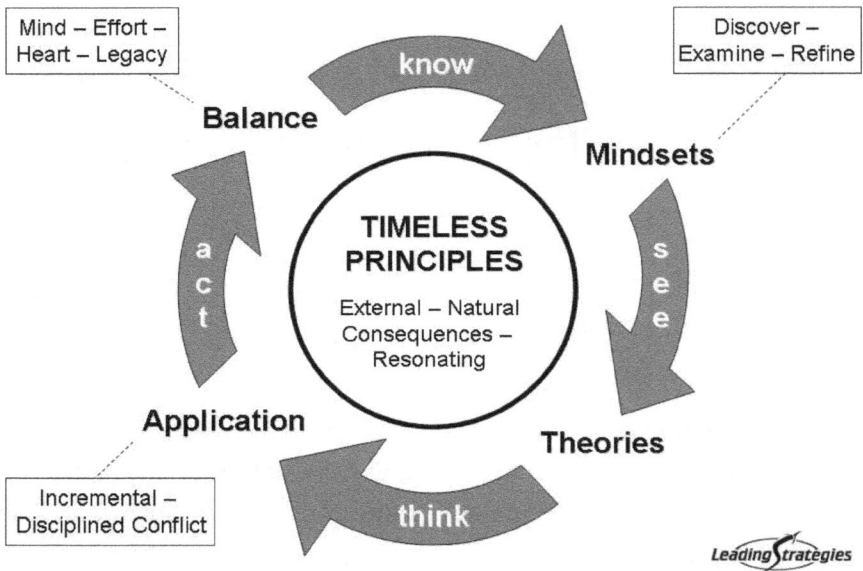

Responsiveness

One of the intriguing discoveries in the process of writing this book is the importance of responding at all levels. The levels span from responsiveness to self, others and to the marketplace. The industrial age mindset did not demand as much response at least in the way we consider it today. In the early days of building things in an assembly line fashion, the most valuable feedback needed was knowledge of demand. It is legendary of how the Model T Ford was available in only one color. Today, customers no longer participate in a market model simply because it exists as there are far too many other options. Responsiveness was needed then as now but the form is different.

Today responsiveness needs to be much more dynamic. The Western insistence for quality and creative solutions promptly marginalizes those who do not respond quickly and deeply enough. This is not unique to for-profit business but is pervasive throughout the cast of organizations. What consumers expect in their cell phones and Blackberries® translates over into what they expect in a volunteer organization or non-profit foundation. It is very much about responsiveness. This expectation impacts every organization in some way. While we can rail against such a demanding mindset, it is reality so we are left with the choice of how to respond, if at all. Interestingly, no response still is a response. You can be sure companies that do not respond well internally behave much the same externally while those with great internal cultures exude warmth and responsiveness to the consumer and it is in their long-term interest to do so. By not responding, we can all but assure ourselves of a diminishing place in the realm of ideas.

However, responsiveness starts with individuals since all organizations are made of people. Do I have the humility to listen to you to strengthen how I see the issue at hand? Can I consistently build trust because my actions are consistently aligned with timeless principles? Can I combine the new information with a solid values foundation in order to produce something better than either of us would have accomplished alone? As go each of us, so goes the respective organizations in which we participate.

No matter what we internally believe about the nobility of our product or service, the responsive cultural student realizes the critical nature of making a difference within a business or agency climate. This enables the student to then communicate the importance of the output in clear language that demonstrates meeting needs. Barring concern for the stakeholders "out there," a business, religious or social agency has a high probability of prematurely fading into history.

Human Leverage Required

As with all theories, finding a way to translate to real and effective action can be quite interesting. Improving culture is all about influence on some scale. Therefore, one key requirement in order for the lessons of this book to take hold is for the cultural student to have influence with at least one other person. This relationship can be formal, informal, peer,

> **If the cultural explorer is unable to influence at least one other person in the group, cultural improvement is impossible.**

subordinate or superior or any combination thereof. The type of connection is not as important as exercising principled influence. Improving culture by its very nature requires leveraging human interaction to begin a deeper look at mindsets, theories, application and balance. This effort will have a corresponding ripple effect throughout any organization if the participants are persistent. If the cultural explorer is unable to influence at least one other person, cultural improvement will not happen despite the best of intentions. If this disappointing turn of events occurs, here are some questions to consider (notice the appearance of "why, what and how" questions).

- Why do I not have any apparent influence with others?
- What things should I start or stop doing in order to have influence in a principled manner?
- How is my personal credibility? What areas can I improve by cultivating trust?
- Should I stay in the environment to give influence a chance? If so, how long? What indicators do I need to indicate the tender shoots of influence?

The Challenge

Will you embrace the path of leading cultural improvement and actively work to become much better than you are today? Will you seek to live outside a one-person universe and make a difference for a larger enterprise? Will you move beyond a results-only mindset and consider the power of culture influences? Maybe you are well on your way in the leadership continuum. Will you then commit to never tiring of continuous improvement in learning to influence culture? Will you resolve to teach and help others do the same? How well do you see things? What are you confident of knowing? How great can you be in this field of principled living? How effectively will you act to produce outstanding results? Hopefully you regard it as a gift that the answers are in your hands.

Glossary

Balance – The intersection of mind, effort, heart and legacy. The theme is renewal and steps back from the daily grind of work to determine what is best. The mind element is the planner of the bunch. The effort component spends an appropriate amount of time and effort to maintain, renew and re-charge the individual or enterprise. Heart helps maintain a focus that we are always dealing with relationships and it is critical to value people at all levels. Legacy wants to make a difference and leave the business better than how it was found.

Change – Change in methods, techniques or practices all based on timeless principles.

Conscience – An inner voice that helps a person tell the difference between right and wrong. Conscience is much like a muscle in that if it is used regularly, it grows stronger and more sensitive. If conscience is consistently ignored, it will become progressively weaker and may disappear altogether in extreme cases. Using conscience requires a person to take a momentary, internal pause to make the moral decision.

Culture – A collection of two or more individuals who exhibit personality, preferences, traits, values and a general way of being and doing.

Effective – Effectiveness is doing the right things for the right reasons especially in human relationships.

Efficient – To be efficient is to squeeze the most output from a given resource, work through a process quickly or follow a method to complete the objective in the fewest steps. Efficiency is focused on things.

Leadership – A way of thinking, a principled approach to life, a healthy respect for the long-term and always focused on building trust. Leadership is more than a position.

Leverage – This concept means every pound of effort yields a greater than usual result. Just as a mechanical lever allows movement of relatively heavier objects with a smaller, leverage in a cultural or leadership context identifies those activities that either impact several other areas at the same time or one area in great measure.

Mindset – A paradigm, mental map, way of seeing, perception; this building block is the basis for any decision making.

Mission – The reason something exists; at its essence, what are you doing and why?

Paradigm – Please see mindset definition above.

Systemic – A systemic perspective looks at the larger context of an issue for greater awareness of actions and reactions. Systemic thinking is about linkage to many other things.

Timeless Principles – Timeless principles are natural laws that govern human behavior accepted by most healthy societies. These are external to us in that we cannot change, delete or add to them and the natural, long-term consequences are also out of our control. Principles resonate with the majority of people as true. Examples of timeless principles include excellence, respect, integrity, courage, kindness, loyalty, commitment, honesty, service, humor, forgiveness, teamwork, renewal, patience, faith, persistence, charity, diligence, and consideration.

Values – Those things important to us; how we conduct business.

Vision – The ultimate destination for an individual, family or enterprise. What is our overarching and longest-term objective?

Suggested Reading

Bennis, Warren (1989). *On Becoming a Leader*. Perseus Books.

Collins, Jim and Porras, Jerry (1997). *Built to Last*. New York, NY. HarperCollins Publishers Inc.

Collins, Jim (2001). *Good to Great*. New York, NY. HarperCollins Publishers Inc.

Goleman, Daniel and Boyatzis, Richard and McKee, Annie (2002). *Primal Leadership*. Boston, MA. Harvard Business Press.

Hammer, Michael (2001). *The Agenda*. New York, NY. Three Rivers Press.

Khalsa, Mahan (1999). *Let's Get Real or Let's Not Play*. Salt Lake City, UT. Franklin Covey Co.

Kotter, John P. (1996). *Leading Change*. Boston, MA. Harvard Business School Press.

Tichy, Noel (1997). *The Leadership Engine*. New York, NY. HarperCollins Publishers Inc.

Tichy, Noel (2002). *The Cycle of Leadership*. New York, NY. HarperCollins Publishers Inc.

Ulrich, Dave and Zenger, Jack and Smallwood, Norm (1999). *Results-Based Leadership*. Boston, MA. Harvard Business Press.

Reference

Andersen, Hans Christian (2004). *The Emperor's New Clothes.* Boston, Massachusetts. Houghton Mifflin Company.

Mike Friesen is a former F-4/F-15 pilot and finance officer who served in the Air National Guard and Air Force Reserve for 21 years before retiring at the rank of Lieutenant Colonel. His diverse background also includes work in the banking industry, construction field, and as clergy. Mike holds a B.A. in Management of Human Resources and a Strategic Leadership M.B.A.

Leading Strategies

www.leadingstrategies.net

www.ingramcontent.com/pod-product-compliance
Lightning Source LLC
Chambersburg PA
CBHW031942190326
41519CB00007B/617